TWO SUITCASES
AND A CARRY-ON

NANCY ARCAYNA

Foreword by
Dr. and Master Zhi Gang Sha

BALBOA.PRESS
A DIVISION OF HAY HOUSE

Balboa Press books may be ordered through booksellers or by contacting:

Balboa Press
A Division of Hay House
1663 Liberty Drive
Bloomington, IN 47403
www.balboapress.com
844-682-1282

Because of the dynamic nature of the Internet, any web addresses or links contained in this book may have changed since publication and may no longer be valid. The views expressed in this work are solely those of the author and do not necessarily reflect the views of the publisher, and the publisher hereby disclaims any responsibility for them.

The author of this book does not dispense medical advice or prescribe the use of any technique as a form of treatment for physical, emotional, or medical problems without the advice of a physician, either directly or indirectly. The intent of the author is only to offer information of a general nature to help you in your quest for emotional and spiritual well-being. In the event you use any of the information in this book for yourself, which is your constitutional right, the author and the publisher assume no responsibility for your actions.

Cover Art by Jamm Aquino
Edited by Nadine Kam

Print information available on the last page.

ISBN: 978-1-9822-6312-6 (sc)
ISBN: 978-1-9822-6313-3 (e)

Balboa Press rev. date: 03/04/2021

"Getting over a painful experience is much like crossing monkey bars. You have to let go at some point in order to move forward." ~C.S. Lewis

This book is dedicated to John Paul, my precious son and greatest teacher. You've shown me what true and unconditional love looks like, including the importance of self-love. Thank you for being my greatest gift in life.

CONTENTS

PART 3
You've Got This!

PART 4
The Maintenance Plan

The Road Forward

FOREWORD

Dr. and Master Zhi Gang Sha
Master Sha is the author of 25 books, 11 of which are New York Times bestsellers. Learn more about his worldwide teachings at www.drsha.com

Nancy Arcayna interviewed me during my first visit to Honolulu when I introduced my teachings and my new "Love, Peace and Harmony" song. She was a journalist at the Honolulu Star-Bulletin and was fascinated to learn more about my mission to create love, peace and harmony for humanity, Mother Earth and all universes.

I shared my basic teachings with her about 15 years ago, which definitely piqued her curiosity.

The basics included:

"I have the power to heal myself. You have the power to heal yourself. Together we have the power to heal the world."

Nancy has taken those words to heart during her personal healing story that's on the pages of this book. She may have been a reporter but you can clearly see her passion for healing herself and wanting to help others.

In this book, she shares personal tribulations and how she overcame them through forgiveness and unconditional love for herself and others. She found that love is always the answer.

I'm happy to hear that the teachings and practices made a difference in her life.

My own journey with healing began at an early age. When I was 5 years old, an injection of penicillin left me in a coma. My neighbor was an acupuncturist and put a needle under my nose in the Ren Zhong acupuncture point and woke me up. The near death experience led me on a path of helping others to heal. I studied tai chi at the age of 6 and qigong at age 10. I've also mastered the art of Shaolin Kung fu, I Ching and Feng Shui in addition to becoming a doctor of traditional Chinese medicine, a medical doctor, an herbalist and acupuncturist.

We look for quick fixes for symptoms but true healing requires integration of physical, spiritual, mental and emotional well-being. All sickness occurs on a cellular level due to energy and spiritual blockages, but there's a spiritual solution to every challenge that exists. When we offer unconditional love, we receive many blessings for health, relationships, finances and success.

To love unconditionally has been the highest calling from teachers of all traditions throughout history.

If you want to know if a pear is sweet, taste it. If you want to know the power of unconditional love, experience it.

Always remember that love melts all blockages and transforms all life.

Many Blessings,
Dr. and Master Zhi Gang Sha

PART 1

THE STRUGGLE IS REAL, OR IS IT?

CHAPTER 1

THE DARK AND DOWNWARD SPIRAL

During my darkest days, my mind was filled with dreams about walking along the majestic black lava rock cliffs that met the ocean of turquoise and blues and just stepping off. On more than one occasion, I imagined myself being consumed by the waves that enamour me with their beauty. The water swirling around me in a magical dance. These waves would take away my pain and put a permanent end to my suffering.

These dark thoughts somehow provided a glimmer of light. The idea of not feeling the pain was exhilarating. Thankfully my thoughts weren't followed by action. When I was on the rare flip side and experienced good days, I was at the other end of the spectrum, and was able to feel hope and see the possibilities that life has to offer. It was a hard road and a slippery slope as I worked at finding balance, finding connection, and finding my way back to trusting the universe and believing in myself.

Moments of impact define who we are. We can't always control or predict how these moments will affect us. Sometimes it's best to let the pieces fall where they may and prepare for the next collision or explosion.

If it's one incident, we typically push through, but when hit by a string of unpleasant events, it can lead to a downward spiral that has you feeling like you're falling into the darkness of a bottomless pit. And eventually you hit bottom.

Hitting rock bottom is an overwhelming state of affairs. It leaves one questioning things like whether it's better to live or die or would it have been better not to have been born in the first place. Darkness can be all consuming if you're unable to focus on the light at the end of the tunnel.

Focusing on the good stuff sounds simple enough. You've heard all of the suggestions or statements that are intended to push you in a more positive direction such as finding that glimmer of hope, counting your blessings or the stark reality that it can always be worse. These are not typically helpful statements for someone that's experiencing a downward spiral. I can attest to that. As one who was wallowing in the darkness, I can say without question that positive affirmations or looking for a worst-case scenario, is not the answer. If you're like me, you'll probably not be in the best position to try and trump someone else's demise. In fact, there is no room to even comprehend someone else's misfortune.

It's as if you're falling deeper into despair and just when you think it could not get any worse, it does. You succumb to the darkness because it's the easiest thing to do at the time.

The good news is, when you hit rock bottom, there's nowhere to go but up. You've spiraled down and surrendered to the darkness. There's really no lower spot to go.

Believe me, I've been there. I was immersed in the darkness feeling paralyzed and afraid.

But when this happens and you're in despair, it presents an opportunity for deep transformation. It offers a time when you can reinvent yourself, reconsider dreams and transform all areas of your life. It doesn't happen overnight but it's definitely worth the wait. If you're willing to work through the darkness, amazing things can happen.

I've experienced that rock bottom feeling a couple of times in my life. Once when my longtime marriage was crumbling and divorce was imminent, and another time after I'd gone through a layoff, got rid of all my possessions including a home, all in the name of love, only to end up broke and homeless in the end with all of my belongings condensed into two suitcases and a carry-on bag. Both experiences were epic fails. These are the types of situations that cause one to question their sanity and life choices. Limiting beliefs seep into the mind making it seem like the outcomes were our own fault.

My failures were really lessons in disguise. Lessons, or I'd like to call them gifts, that allowed me to see my self-worth. They became the reasons to provide myself with the self-love that I needed and deserve. Other lessons that presented themselves was the importance of creating boundaries and living in the moment. All of the lessons and gifts provided me the clarity of knowing what was important to me. It set me on a path of creating the life of my dreams.

Don't get me wrong. This place of uncertainty and pain can be paralyzing. It shakes you to the core. It makes you wonder whether you will ever get back up or be whole again. But with trust and faith, and especially love, anything is possible.

Our words and stories may differ but the underlying feelings of pain and suffering are the same. Everyone has a personal story and bouts of joy and sorrow. The idea is to create more joy in life. My story is about having a love affair with myself.

CHAPTER 2

THE DAMAGING SIDE OF DIVORCE

D ivorce is one of those events that can knock you on you on your ass and keep you there for some time. It's an earth-shattering reality that life as you know it has ended. And while divorce can seem like a wonderful thing for a troubled relationship, there is still a lot of emotional baggage that needs to be resolved.

I recall attending events with my ex-husband near the end of my marriage. At one holiday party, I found myself crying, slumped on the bathroom floor at my friend's house. After the meltdown, I washed my face, freshened up, put on a happy face and rejoined the festivities.

Our friends were later surprised when we started the divorce process. By then, I'd become an extremely good actress.

There are so many questions I asked myself after my divorce, such as, "Why aren't you happy when this was what you wanted?"

This is because nobody really wants their love story to end with divorce. None of us get married thinking that our relationship will end up as anything other than "happily ever after." Divorce is unthinkable.

Then there was a sense of personal failure and self-blame. Why couldn't I make it work when we tried so hard to figure out a solution? Was I not satisfied? Was I looking for greener pastures? Was I bored? Was I in love with the feeling of being in love and after two decades, was it just too hard to get that feeling back?

After much contemplation and a whole lot of tears and letting go, I realized that it was none of these things that I feared and dreamed up in my mind. We were in love. We had a beautiful child. Things were wonderful until they weren't. We simply grew apart, which wasn't surprising because from the beginning we were like oil and water, simply not a good mix. My ex-husband wasn't a bad guy. We just didn't fit well together because of cultural differences and life views.

At least that's how I could view it in hindsight. It's easy to focus on the bad and wrongdoings, but through my healing process I found it's better to focus on the positive things; the times when we were happy. Some folks may call this denial but that's so far from the truth.

The specter of divorce can rear its ugly head when partners are feeling wounded. Sometimes children are used as pawns, and security is used as a means of control. Nobody escapes unscathed, but if you keep the ball in your court and control what you can, it may make for an easier exit strategy.

I didn't have a lot of tug-of-war action when going through my divorce, but the disappointment and loss of hopes and dreams loomed over us like a dark cloud that threatened to pummel us at any moment with a myriad of emotions from anger to grief.

These feelings could apply to any relationship breakup, not just a marriage, and the wounds are rarely superficial.

There's a lot more lost during a divorce than lost love. For many or most, it includes a breakdown of the nuclear family, a division of extended family and friends, distribution of belongings collected over the years, all imbued with memories.

For some, divorce is a financial disaster. Others experience a loss of self identity. Some women may have never worked outside of the home and find the prospect of looking for a job terrifying.

I've found that resolution of these issues and healing comes in several layers over time. Just when I thought I had overcome one trauma, I'd get triggered and have to deal with it all over again on a deeper level.

That's never a fun experience. But if you can hang in there, work through your emotions and not get trapped by them, you'll grow and become a stronger person.

My belief is that confronting your pain is the only way to release the hurt or pain and alleviate yourself from carrying around the baggage. Sure, you can try to ignore a problem or pretend it doesn't exist, but if you don't deal with the issues and release painful thoughts, they will haunt you in future relationships or life events. And who wants to keep reliving pain?

One of the biggest obstacles in my journey was fear. I had fears of financial security, fears of being unlovable, fears of being alone, fears of losing everything, fears of being homeless, and the list goes on. Eventually, all of my fears came to fruition. It was like I manifested my worst nightmare. As I lived through the nightmare, solutions were presented that helped me to slowly rebuild my life. I felt broken and each time I made a little progress, I'd pick up another piece of myself and continue to put the pieces back together. It was only an illusion that I was not whole, for I was never broken. I was simply being transformed.

So remember to breathe and give yourself some grace when going through difficult transitions. More importantly, be reminded that there's no timetable for grief and while you can easily let some things go, other things may take longer to heal. And, it's all OK.

CHAPTER 3

DECLUTTERING MY LIFE

D ivorce or any sort of breakup brings change and downsizing may be among the issues that need to be addressed.

Rationally, downsizing simply involves sorting, organizing, decision making and disposing of things no longer needed or wanted. It sounds simple enough but for many, such change is uncomfortable.

Downsizing means walking away from things that are familiar. And although it has positive results and a sense of freedom in the end, the emotional toll is inevitable.

Many of my belongings held precious family memories with my son but it was in my best interest to downsize my life, even though I didn't feel ready to part with treasured belongings. Reminiscing over mementos collected over the course of my marriage was the very thing I was trying to avoid.

As I sorted through each item, I felt like I was chipping away at myself. Every ordinary item in the house seemed to hold a memory, positive or negative, and I needed to decide if the memory would be kept, tossed or recycled.

Feelings of profound grief needed to be addressed as I was faced with losing what used to be. Some objects provided painful memories of lost love, hopes and dreams and the realization of a family torn apart by divorce. One would assume that it's easier to let these things go, but nonetheless, emotions ran high.

The kept items needed to be minimal because I was condensing my life. All of my belongings needed to fit into two suitcases and a carry-on bag so that I would be able to tote everything around with me. Fitting the contents of a three-bedroom house into three pieces of luggage was utterly overwhelming.

The cookies for Santa plate, the Mickey Mouse ears, my favorite books, letters and cards from loved ones, many from those who had passed away, were among the items that didn't make the cut. Practicality was more important than sentiment. It had to be if I was planning on living the transient lifestyle that I'd been dreaming about for so long.

The divorce had shaken me and left me financially distraught. I had a house that I couldn't afford but was managing. But I was only managing because I had dug a hole for myself and was extremely deep in debt.

I needed my job more than ever but I'd lost the passion under poor management and was going through the daily grind feeling physically sick, emotionally drained and spiritually depleted. When a voluntary layoff opportunity was presented, I jumped at the chance. It provided a glimmer of hope during some dark days. The mere thought of leaving my 9-to-5 prison gave me an immense sense of freedom. I was ready to see what evolved as I took a leap of faith.

I'd already been in a new relationship for two years and nearly half of that time had been long distance. My new plan of transient living would provide an opportunity to remove the long-distance aspect. I was head over heels, so why not?

I hadn't expected to find love so quickly after my divorce; well it had been four years, but it didn't feel long. My heart was fragile but my new man made me feel like I was on top of the world. I was the center of his universe and he was mine. He accepted me "as is" and provided me with all of the things that had been lacking in my marriage. I felt like he was putting some of my broken pieces back together and helping me to mend. I felt whole again. I had worked on my spiritual development and it seemed as if it had finally paid off. Love had made the process of downsizing a little bit easier.

Many of my friends commented on my downsizing stating that it must be wonderful and freeing. So I'd suggest that they do it with my help, which never happened and thankfully the comments stopped. More than 15,000 photographs were scanned and all of the originals were left behind. My son's early artwork pieces were too big for the scanner and I ran out of time before I needed to move, so those are just mere memories in my mind. But I don't miss stuff, and I'm glad that I accomplished my goal, even if it was a gut-wrenching and emotionally draining project.

"Let go," I told myself. Simply let go. They are just things; just a bunch of stuff. The memories remain in my heart and in my head. I didn't need trophies and keepsakes to prove anything. But melancholy set in on more than one occasion during the letting-go process.

Deciding what to keep and what to discard had me trapped on an emotional roller coaster throughout the endeavor. It became easier to let things go as time passed by. Three small bins containing my son's baby and childhood mementos were stored for him but my personal belongings had to fit into the suitcases.

I loved the family house and thought it was going to be my forever home. Saying goodbye was not easy. It was where we were going to set our roots. After the painstaking review of my life in this house, and placing value on each item, roots were not something I desired anymore. I wanted freedom. The freedom to move around and see new things, experience different places and pursue passions. I was no longer a caged bird. I didn't view myself as stuck anymore. I was free. I could soar and had it all planned out.

CHAPTER 4

LOOKING FOR LOVE IN ALL THE WRONG PLACES

Prior to the plan, you could say that I kissed a lot of toads.

After being in a longtime marriage, the thought of being alone was terrifying. When I got married, it was supposed to be forever, and here I was starting over at square one.

I found love again about four years after my divorce but prior to that, I was hopping from one relationship to another. My choice in men proved that I wasn't ready to start over. Time needed to heal some of the deep wounds. Instead of taking time to heal, I created more wounds because of my fear of being alone.

Since self-love was nonexistent in my life, I needed the love and adoration of another person. But the relationships I found didn't have any chance of becoming long term commitments, and at that time I welcomed that temporary quality. It was as if I was void of emotion. Or maybe it was because I was filled with so many undesirable emotions that I had built walls around my heart.

Online dating was the norm but it was not fun. The men I encountered always seemed to lie about their height and age. I suppose age is something that you can play with but no one can be deceptive about height discrepancies once you meet. Men I know complained of similar lies from women they met online. And if they lie about facts that can be easily checked, who's to say they aren't lying about more major aspects of their lives, from work life to family to love relationships? And yes, there are quite a few marrieds looking for hookups online.

Whatever the case, online dating can be disastrous. I have a friend who started profusely sweating and had a panic attack while telling me about one of her horrible dating experiences. She had agreed to join her date for breakfast but didn't set up a quick exit strategy. The waitress had forgotten to put in their order, which prolonged the agony. She never put herself in that spot again. If you find yourself on a really bad date, don't stick around. Be honest and leave.

My exit strategy was always to meet for a quick coffee or drink, and get out fast if need be, after experiencing my share of really bad first dates. Many men post old photos in which they looked much better than their current state. Men my age—who are old, bald and fat—still want to date someone who looks like a Barbie doll, which is hilarious. The men who wanted to date me were much younger than me, and I didn't like the idea of being called a cougar.

It made sense to try to hit a sweet spot between men my age and those my son's age. I decided that it would be best to date men about 10 years younger than myself, which at that time was 36. They were equals in accomplishment and intellect, and they seemed to have fewer hang-ups than older men.

There were a few dates that made it past the first meeting. Fireman and German Guy were in this mix. I preferred not to refer to my partners by their names when discussing them with friends. I made up nicknames, which increased the sense of detachment, like a farmer who tends to animals and refrains from giving them names to avoid becoming attached to them as pets. That's kind of how I felt about these men.

I'd find myself with good looking, fit men that had little else to offer me besides being eye candy and meeting my sexual needs.

The Fireman was one of my first attempts at getting back into the dating scene. We formed a friends-with-benefits style of relationship. We watched movies, had casual conversations over a glass of wine and spent time together, but I knew from the start that it couldn't go anywhere. We had nothing in common besides our desires in the bedroom. He was tall, dark and handsome; a sexy fireman, but that was about it. We had no deep conversations, he didn't make me laugh and he didn't have the qualities I was seeking in a partner. But he got me feeling comfortable in my own skin again.

We eventually parted ways. I felt a bit heartbroken, which didn't really make sense, so I quickly moved on with German Guy. I was in a bad place when I met him. I was going through some dark times, juggling some family issues, and I was not in a good state of mind to pursue a relationship. But he intrigued me.

He may have been a spy. Although I say this jokingly, it could have been the truth since he would disappear for a couple weeks to go on an assignment to Morocco or Turkey. He had a thick German accent and worked for the American government. I'll never be sure because I didn't take any time to get concrete details about him. If I didn't want to get attached, it was best to have less information. We were together for a little over a year.

None of my friends even knew about the relationship until after it ended and he moved out of state. I made sure that our intimacy remained on a superficial level. There were no sleepovers and no dates outside of the home. It was a "Netflix and Chill" style relationship. He continually told me that I "was a good woman" and I replied that "he wasn't boyfriend material." Basically, I treated him like a sex toy.

He definitely fulfilled a fantasy. He was like a bad boy straight out of a James Bond movie. He was tall and strong with piercing light brown eyes and a slight frown. And he had an amazing body. He thrilled me and got me out of my head, which I needed in a bad way.

We would connect almost every night and have sex, but again, there were no sleepovers, no deep intimacy and although we had amazing chemistry, there was no real connection.

Then there was GI Joe, who is almost not worth mentioning but clearly reveals my state of mind at the time. He was much younger than me and way too needy. Spending time with him required way too much work and ended after a few weeks on the day that he jumped over my fence instead of going through the gate. He was always hungry like a child after a long day at school. I felt like he was more of a burden than anything else. He was proof that good looks aren't enough. I had to question my shallowness when dealing with these men.

They all had abs of steel and were definitely worth a head turn, but there wasn't much substance. It was really more about me keeping my heart safe and avoiding more pain.

Sleeping with these men was not getting me any closer to finding love again. It actually served as a barrier and kept love out of reach.

Obviously it was too painful to find love again so I made sure that I'd choose men that were emotionally unavailable because I was emotionally unavailable.

People who are emotionally unavailable often have trust issues because of things that happened in their past. I was full of anxiety and anxiety is all about fear. There's the fear or intimacy because getting close to someone could lead to pain. The fear of being exposed as a fraud or judged in any way also plays into being emotionally unavailable. It's also hard to place depth and trust in the relationship if you're a people pleaser and care about the opinions of others.

If you've ever experienced what it's like to be in a relationship with someone emotionally unavailable, you'll understand the pain that it can cause. During my marriage, I often felt as if my spouse was emotionally unavailable and it was extremely painful and caused deep feelings of loneliness.

There's deep pain involved when you're not able to get close to the one you love. There was always an excuse, or something else that needed more attention. He was inept when it came to talking about feelings or our relationship. Sometimes he appeared angry or would use criticism to create distance, which left me feeling unloved, rejected, alone and depressed. It's normal to feel lonely when you're alone but it's tougher to feel lonely when someone is lying next to you. The divorce left me feeling numb. I made myself emotionally unavailable and sought out partners that didn't mind.

After things ended with the fence jumper, I decided to take a break and stop dating for some time. I'd keep myself busy with work and other projects. It was easier than trying to weed through the masses to try and find a new man to nickname and keep at arm's length.

If you find yourself in a similar circumstance, make sure that you evaluate your motivations for seeking a partner. It's important to be realistic about what you're doing to ensure that you're not going in blindly. Potential hazards could cause more harm than good.

Finding true love seemed to be a Herculean task, and to be honest, I was terrified of putting myself in the position of getting hurt again. The idea of being stuck in a relationship that was going nowhere, where I'd fallen in love, was almost more grim than being alone. So my decision to remain single kept me feeling safe.

CHAPTER 5

FINDING LOVE AGAIN

The old saying goes that when one door closes another one opens. But if you turn back and try to open the closed door, you may miss out on a multitude of opportunities.

I believe everything happens for a reason and that there are no accidents or coincidences. On many occasions, it may be challenging to see a good reason for the bad things that may happen to you, but down the road you will and you'll be able to appreciate why circumstances unfolded as they did. If you keep an open mind, opportunities will present themselves.

It's not always easy to remain open when dealing with matters of the heart. Often when we are hurt, we build walls and barriers of protection that need to be broken down before love can enter our lives.

After a long marriage and experiencing the drudgery of divorce, I wasn't in a hurry to put my heart out there, which was apparent in the way I'd been handling my love life for four years. I wondered whether it was even possible to find love again. All of my horrible dates didn't instill much faith in the process.

And then it happened...just like that. I wasn't looking. I didn't want it. I couldn't bear the thought of being hurt again.

But, more frightened by the prospect of being alone than broken-hearted, I got sucked in by the allure of dating apps once again. This time I was looking for a relationship with an emotionally available partner. By fate, I accidentally swiped in the wrong direction and ended up in contact with a man I intended to pass over. We started to communicate, so I gave it a shot.

He lived nearly 5,000 miles away. We were an ocean and continent apart since I was in Hawaii. We communicated for six weeks via texts and phone and video calls before we met in person. By then, I already knew that I liked him. He was charming and sweet. On the day that he landed in Hawaii for his job, we met for our first official date. It was a delightful evening. We had great chemistry and I spent time with him every day thereafter.

There were dinners, walks, sunsets, drives around beautiful and romantic scenic spots and deep intimacy. When he left almost a year later to travel to a new location for his job, my heart was already "all in" and there was no turning back. We maintained a long-distance relationship for the next three years.

He traveled regularly for work and would come back to Honolulu now and then, but these trips always ended with a tearful goodbye. He dutifully texted and we talked and video-chatted during our time apart but I wanted more. He promised that we would be together one day. We would make it work.

The discussions of being together in the same location kept me going. We talked about it endlessly, fantasized about the possibilities, and made promises that we would definitely figure out how to make it work.

After leaving my job of nearly two decades, moving out of my house and condensing all of my belongings into the suitcases, I was finally ready for the next steps. I had tied up all of those loose ends and was anticipating this next exciting chapter. I was overjoyed that I'd found love again.

He was uprooted regularly and sent to new locations for work assignments, so friends who were suspicious about his home status questioned my sanity. They would ask me, "Don't you need roots?" I smiled on the inside and would say, "I have roots. They're always within me...in my heart."

With that mindset, every place I visit feels like home.

When I was finally physically and mentally ready to make the move, my move was put on hold. He was on another job and there were some issues that made it a bad time for me to join him. I had to wait once again. I decided to head to the mainland and do some traveling before our rendezvous. Making the move and leaving everything familiar behind was challenging and much more emotional than I expected, so I made a decision to do some exploring before we connected. Everything seemed to be unfolding perfectly, because I was ready. I was headed on a grand adventure.

My trek began when I hopped on a plane with my whole life packed into two suitcases and carry-on. A couple months into my travels, my boyfriend was retrieving me from the airport. Finally! We were in the same apartment and it was to be a permanent situation. We had lived together in Honolulu for a few weeks here and a couple months there, but this was going to be different. I wouldn't have to think about the dreaded end date of his work assignment. There wouldn't be any more painful goodbyes. Being away for nearly a year and only sneaking a week in here and there would be a thing of the past. When the end date came, I'd be moving to the next location, too. I became quite astute at making temporary locales feel like home. Everything was absolutely wonderful and all felt right in the world. I was working on my writing and other projects while he was on the job. I had been patient and the wait was finally over. I'd opened my heart to let love in and it had paid off.

Love has a funny way of sneaking up on us. It hits us when we least expect it. I had told him that I wasn't ready for a relationship but here we were, nearly four years later, in the same time zone, side by side. How nice it was to wake up and not be alone anymore. I was definitely smiling and laughing a lot more. It was apparent that I was lovable. I deserved to be happy. I was in love. But sadly, this state was fleeting.

The proper statement would be that I laughed lots until I cried. And once the floodgates opened, it felt like I cried several bucketfuls of tears.

CHAPTER 6

DECEIT AND HEARTBREAK

Trust between couples, or any two people for that matter, should be relatively simple. When you trust someone, you can depend on them. They're reliable. It's easy to feel safe, both emotionally and physically. Trust provides the faith that you have in someone to remain loyal and love you. In a partner situation, this person becomes your confidant, your lover, your advisor.

Trust is among the most important foundational building blocks in any relationship. Some telltale signs that your partner is trustworthy include their willingness to open up and be vulnerable. It's OK to fully put yourself out there because you feel safe and secure. All relationships need a foundation of trust if they want to sustain for the long term. Without trust, one can't maintain a healthy relationship.

Once in that safe zone where you think you've found someone you feel you could entrust with your life, finding out this person you know, love and deemed trustworthy betrayed you is devastating. A spider web of lies turned my world upside down. My heart might as well have stopped beating at the moment I learned I had been living a lie for four years.

In my situation, we openly shared our feelings on matters large and small, but within months of living together full-time, I learned there were lots of omissions on my partner's side.

When one woman's name kept popping up on his phone, he claimed that she was a casual friend. But it happened so often that one day while he was sleeping, I messaged her and was shocked to learn that she had been, and was still, his girlfriend. They had met nearly eight years ago, double the time that I had been with him. It was an earth-shattering realization. I'd condensed all of my life into a couple of pieces of luggage for this?

The "other woman" and I video chatted for a few hours on the following day after the initial text that I'd sent, acting as a mirror of pain for one another. We compared notes and cried and sometimes sat in silence for moments because it was just too painful to speak. He had served as a father figure to her children, which was even worse. Everything suddenly seemed surreal. We decided to confront him together on the video call so that he wouldn't be able to feed us more lies.

"I'm really not feeling well. Could you please come home for lunch," I asked him. He was reluctant since he was on his lunch break and texting her while we were on the call. He used these times to talk with her for longer periods of time, so that everything seemed normal and OK on her side, too.

He told me that he was only casual friends with this woman and that they didn't engage in conversation very often. He made her out to be very unimportant in his life. But that obviously wasn't the case.

He was so extremely angry and in my face when I told him that I'd reached out to her so I really didn't need any more confirmation of the truth. His anger was frightening.

When he arrived home during his lunch break and I turned the phone around, he had to look at both of our faces. He was immediately angered and ready to walk out the door but we needed an explanation. His response to me was, "I should have left you."

Maybe those words were for her benefit, since I'd already started packing my bags. She sat there dumbfounded, not able to speak, as she had to look at us standing in the apartment where we were living together. He had lied to her, saying that I was a crazy and delusional ex-girlfriend that was no longer in his life. Yet there I was standing next to the table where we ate dinner each night and next to the bed that we slept in each night. He started crying and apologizing to both of us.

The pain for me was immeasurable and his apologies were hollow. In my opinion, he wasn't sorry that he hurt us. He was sorry that he got caught. We were both collateral damage in the grand scheme of things. We were both numb. Why didn't we see the red flags?

It's important to pay attention to personal relationships and take note of the person's physical presence when you're together. Awareness is key because energy doesn't lie and there were many red flags that should have been apparent. For instance, we were living in close proximity to his family but I'd never met them, not even his son or parents. He had said that he was able to spend a couple of weeks with them before I arrived, but in actuality, they didn't even know he was nearby.

Red flags are often a part of romance scams, whether it's toying with matters of the heart or getting duped to send money or comply in some other manner. Endless news reports of dating scammers have been documented where partners are convinced to send funds so that they can set up a future with their partner. As if wearing blinders, victims are unaware that anything is wrong until their love interest disappears along with their money.

After my relationship ended, the warning signs became crystal clear. He was constantly on his phone and carried it with him at all times. It was rarely in my sight and pretty much off limits. He was defensive sometimes when asked questions about his actions but he had a logical answer or excuse for everything. Being an honest person, one doesn't expect to deal with a pathological liar. That's what I had. I'd been lied to every day for nearly four years. The heartbreak was beyond devastating.

After the discovery of betrayal, my feelings of anger, hurt, bewilderment, betrayal and numbing shock were overwhelming and almost too much to bear. I had arranged for a flight back to the islands a few days after the confrontation and had a complete mental breakdown prior to my departure. For days I would fall to my knees crying and just lie on the floor in a heap. I threw my suitcases around as if to curse them for bringing me to this situation. My fate made me angry at God. And I was especially angry at myself.

Breathing and simple tasks suddenly felt daunting and difficult. I couldn't eat for a couple of months. I didn't have the energy or will to nourish myself. I did some liquid cleanses at a doctor's suggestion just to get some nutrients. When I asked why I couldn't eat food or keep anything down since this hadn't happened before, my doctor's response was, "At the moment, you don't care if you live or die."

This statement was true and hard hitting.

Taking a partner's love for granted because you're in it for the long haul is a common occurrence. And why shouldn't it be? Love and trust are the minimal expectations of a relationship.

My whole heart had been handed over to my boyfriend on a platter. He had proclaimed to love me with all of his heart. I'd trusted him completely and he simply wasn't worthy of that.

I'd somehow lost myself in the process of loving someone, but it wasn't a complete loss. He had healed some of the old wounds from my broken marriage by saying all of the right things.

Unfortunately, he forgot to mention that another woman received that same loving kindness. I was extremely disheartened with my findings. He was my one and only and I thought I was his. During my discussions with her, she felt the same way about their relationship. It was just sad. I'll never know the full extent of his lies and it's not really necessary. The only necessity was moving forward again and healing my own heart.

For he may as well have stomped on my heart and crushed it right then and there to stop it from beating and enduring so much pain. It would have spared me a lot of heartache.

I'd been overjoyed that I'd found love in my life. It was refreshing to feel those butterflies again and delight in those feelings of a new and loving relationship.

After all, he was the reason for my "two suitcases and a carry-on" theme. I took a whole house of memories and condensed it so that all of my belongings would fit in the suitcases that I would be toting around. I'd be toting them around to be with him.

I'd made the big move from Hawaii because I was ecstatic to finally have removed the long distance aspect from our relationship but also fascinated by the idea of exploring new places and meeting new people. It seemed like the perfect plan. And it was the perfect plan, again, until it wasn't.

My situation was mind-boggling and incomprehensible. Everything had seemed so ideal. My long term planning had finally come to fruition. As a couple living together, we shared beautiful homemade dinners together with interesting conversations and profound intimacy. I suppose it's because he had a lot of practice. He was living a double life where he would tell this other woman the same things he was telling me. He was self-centered and selfish. Not only was he carrying on with at least the two of us, but he was also still married. After calling his wife to apologize since he had told me that he was divorced, she confirmed that he had been carrying on with numerous women for more than a decade and that she had only stuck around for financial security. She expressed that I wasn't the first woman to call her and that I wouldn't be the last.

Our conversation was painful. I got the feeling that she thought he was just having one night stands, or flings and not full-fledged emotional relationships. The thought that he had been doing this to his own wife and family for more than a decade was appalling. I walked away immediately and wouldn't have been able to stay no matter which of those circumstances existed. I'd felt "not good enough" for most of my life and him having to have someone else brought that painful realization to the surface. How could I be drawn into this romance scam?

He always had trouble sleeping and now I understood why. Juggling so many different relationships must have been challenging. It must have taken a lot of organization to keep all of it straight.

This man's phone served as a personal dating site where he added women from all over the globe. He kept them on the hook, some in deep, committed long-distance relationships like ours, so that he could tap into that list as he traveled for work.

It must have taken great effort to hide and keep up the communication with all of us. I suppose when he ran out to take calls, always saying it was his son, and had a tight hold on his phone, that deep down, I should have realized that there was a problem. But I was deeply in love and he was my one and only so I ignored and overlooked these actions. I wasn't ready to let go, most likely because I still had my own demons to face, and wasn't practicing self-love.

I'd learned long ago that you can't control anyone else. You only have control over what you can do, how you can respond and your reaction to others and situations.

The betrayal completely blindsided me. He didn't look like a player. In fact, he was quite ordinary looking, short and far from drop dead gorgeous. He didn't demonstrate player qualities but I guess that made it easier to pull it all off and to keep up his ever growing web of lies. It was his appeal and charm that got you. He said all of the right things to make a woman feel loved, beautiful and perfect "as is."

The growing self-esteem I felt from hearing those words was probably one of the few things I gained from the relationship, but it was a major gain. I needed it at the time. I'd spent 20 years in a marriage where I never felt good enough. My flaws were always pointed out. It was refreshing to feel like I didn't need to change a thing. I was finally perfect "as is."

After all of the fallout, that esteem didn't get torn down, and for that, I am grateful. It actually helped to propel me on a journey of self-love. This journey helped me to face my demons and overcome my fears. This was the gift. It didn't feel like a gift in the beginning, but it allowed me to grow exponentially.

The person that I'd fallen in love with had no more place in my life but it didn't reduce the hurt; it still felt immensely painful. On some level, he really couldn't help his actions. And no, I'm not making excuses. There is no excuse for the kind of behavior that caused so much pain and grief for others. But from what he shared, and I believe was true, parts of his upbringing left a deep painful scar, one that was hidden but always present, waiting to resurface. He deeply needed the approval and adoration of women which he's spent a lifetime pursuing. Yet, none of us could ever fill that void.

Most people could not understand how I could be compassionate toward someone who had just turned my life upside down. I'd literally hit rock bottom—with no home, no money, no job and now, no relationship. But I had been on a spiritual journey prior to meeting him and had lots of tools in my tool box. I was not going to change the person that I had become because of the pain that he had caused. He had to have been an extremely broken person to be able to treat people this way. It would take a pretty messed up individual to destroy countless other people's hopes and dreams. It was all on him and had nothing to do with what we did or didn't do.

His lack of integrity was not going to hinder my kindness, though. I didn't want his actions to leave me bitter so I took my power back.

I was kind to him, his girlfriend and his wife. It was that kindness and compassion towards everyone involved in the situation that allowed me to move forward and reclaim the life that I want to live. It helped me to grow in so many ways. Kindness requires great strength. Compassion isn't always easy in these types of circumstances. It takes effort, especially when hit with a tsunami of emotions from regret and sorrow to grief and anger. The waves of emotion and confusion were uncontrollable and unpredictable at times. Heartache has a way of making things appear surreal. I had to question what happened. It just didn't seem real. How could it be?

It was definitely real and extremely painful but each place and person that I've encountered along this part of my journey, left me with something. I learned to find the gift or lesson in all of my encounters.

And one of my biggest takeaways from this ordeal was seeing myself perfect "as is" and knowing that his words only assisted to steer my views of self in a positive direction.

In the end, it was all on me. We can all be strong or weak, happy or sad, or living in a place of fear or love. We all get to decide. We can change our thoughts and perspectives at any time. Happiness was my choice. And although it didn't happen overnight, and took many months for me to even begin to recover from this ordeal, it still happened.

The realization that I could shift my reality at any given moment has been a saving grace. It doesn't mean that the seriousness or pain of the situation is diminished or will disappear, but being open to the shift in consciousness can be a life changer. You're already on the path of healing when you simply acknowledge that changing your thoughts can change your situation and your life. You're one thought or decision away from a different life.

As you learn to love yourself more, entertaining thoughts that hurt you or keep you stuck will become unacceptable. A friend who was a MMA fighter once told me that it didn't matter how many times that you get knocked down. He said what was important is that the time it took to get back up was shortened. This applies well to life. We always have setbacks and things that throw us off balance. But if you can find the tools to get back up as quickly as possible, it makes a world of difference for your happiness and well-being.

Remember to give yourself some grace and know that it takes time to recover from painful circumstances. Grace and being kind to yourself is a form of self-love. Imagine the love that you'd provide a friend in a similar circumstance and treat yourself that way.

During these months of healing, my thoughts were dizzying. If I'd not afforded myself some grace, the recovery process would have taken much longer.

PART 2

TAKE THAT FIRST STEP

CHAPTER 7

SPIRITUAL GROWTH DOESN'T LOOK PRETTY

Images of a yogi or zen master sitting in silence come to mind when I think about spirituality. It seems like if you follow their path, you'll get there, too. And you do. My journey just didn't appear as calm or pretty.

The realization hit hard. My spiritual path was not a straight line that would have allowed me to simply move from point A to point B.

Instead, my path would prove windy and curvy, with many steps backward, like the scribbled artwork of a 2- or 3-year-old. I dabbled in energy work, varied healing modalities, essential oils and anything similar that might lift my spirits.

Sometimes my pursuit of joy would only dredge up old wounds. In searching for happiness, I was forced to confront my past failures and found myself frequently reliving the hurts, leaving me feeling worse.

After contemplation, I realized that I'd just reached a deeper layer of issues that needed attention. Peeling away the layers helped me to feel lighter and freer. I may have been moving backward and in circles, but any which way is OK, as long as you're taking steps to inch forward. Even with baby steps, you'll reach your goal eventually.

I'll say it many times over: there is no timetable for overcoming grief and heartache. But time does have a way of pushing us toward healing.

The profound hurts I experienced forced me to dig deep. It caused me to evaluate how I was living my life and how I was part of the problem. Even though I'd grown up going to church every Sunday and to vacation Bible studies on school holidays, I'd been disconnected from God and all things spiritual for most of my life. The realization of my lack of faith needed to take place before my journey began. If I wanted to walk a spiritual path, an abundance of soul searching was required.

What is a spiritual journey anyway? To some, it might sound like some New Age mumbo jumbo. In actuality, my view of spirituality is about finding out who you really are, what lights you up or or awakens hidden passions. It also allows you to view the problems in your life, such as limiting beliefs or survival mechanisms that might have served you at one point but would be best kicked to the curb during the current stage of your life.

But the main purpose of spirituality is finding connection to a greater power, whether that be God, the universe, Mother Nature or your higher self. It doesn't matter what you choose to call it. What's important is feeling a sense of connectedness to everyone and everything around you.

Life is full of unexpected ups and downs. Choices and more choices are continually thrown at us. We may make the wrong decisions or question our beliefs based on societal pressures, but once we start soul-searching, decision-making comes easier and what others think matters less. When we are feeling disconnected and driven by emotions, it's challenging to make the kind of clear decisions that would allow us to jump off the hamster wheel of life and stop running in circles.

But don't think of the spiritual journey as one with a singular destination. Instead, the road is winding and involves pursuit of answers to questions that continually arise. It's a never-ending adventure.

My journey ramped up after going through a voluntary layoff at work. After working at a daily newspaper for nearly 20 years, I finally had the time to decompress and reevaluate my life. I was sick and tired of being on autopilot. I was sick and tired of feeling sick and tired. My divorce was finalized and instead of feeling a sense of complete freedom and new possibilities, I was saddled with the extra responsibility of paying a mortgage that I couldn't afford on my own and raising a teenage son with little support. Neither scenario was an easy feat nor much fun, but both provided me with lessons and an opportunity to learn more about myself. It brought me to where I'm at today.

Torn between wanting to live in paradise and knowing that I was digging a deeper hole left me with the realization that downsizing had been necessary. It was my best option, and plus, I'd found love and downsizing would need to happen to move onto the phase of my life.

Condensing my entire home and belongings into two suitcases and a carry-on was the end goal and I'd accomplished it. I couldn't see the point of hanging on to any dead weight. The dead weight at the time included an expensive mortgage that left me over my head in debt and a loveless house that left me with a deep sense of failure and loneliness.

Don't get me wrong. I had plenty of people around me. Wonderful friends supported me through the madness, but no one truly understood what I was going through. Feeling alone became the norm.

Loneliness is an interesting emotion because you can feel lonely even when you're surrounded by people. The connection to source when experiencing these types of feelings is especially important. It's helpful to understand that you're never truly alone.

All of the transitions that I was going through were overwhelming. The process of letting go of all that was familiar was terrifying.

Change can be challenging, scary and extremely sad. I could go through the list of emotions because I felt them all and at varying levels at some point during my journey. It taught me to stand tall despite adversity and circumstances. It also forced me to find the courage it takes to move forward and not remain stagnant.

The situations caused me to have faith even though it felt like my world had bottomed out and there was nothing left for me. I learned to shift my attitude, which had me looking beyond dismal situations toward possibilities that might emerge from continuing my path forward.

I learned to love myself, which had previously been a foreign concept. Self-love and respect are critical to one's well-being.

Along the way, I also learned that mistakes aren't really mistakes. They are just a means to get you moving in a different direction. If you're not failing or making mistakes, chances are that you're not really living life. I'm no longer afraid to fail or make mistakes,

So yes, I've been through a lot, and you probably have, too, but I'm here to remind you that change is the only constant. So being flexible and patient are key components to getting through life. Love, especially self-love, will remove the blockages in life and allow you to move forward.

Bask in the wisdom that you gain along the way and don't sleepwalk through life. Start simple, if need be.

Choosing how you view yourself in the world is an important step. If I had accepted people's judgments of me when I was in deep despair, I'd most likely have stepped off that cliff and ended my pain. So be sure that you're not living by another person's standards when it doesn't feel right for you. Stop comparing yourself to others. Stop judging other people. And more importantly, stop judging yourself harshly. We are often our worst critics.

And remember, don't stop living when painful situations arise. If you need to put up temporary walls, so be it, but work through the mess and break them down in the end.

Life is a gift, so my advice is, don't waste your precious time. Enjoy each and every moment. Learn to embrace life's ups and downs. That way it will be much easier to climb the mountain and get to the other side. Finding the joy and happiness that you deserve will naturally come your way. It all starts with self-love.

CHAPTER 8

JOURNEY OF SELF LOVE

Someone once told me to have a passionate love affair with myself, and that sounded nuts at the time, but now I totally get it.

At the time, right after my divorce, I didn't have a clue what this person had meant. At first thought, it seemed like some sort of pleasantry; simply a nice way to say be alone for a while and take all the time you need to get your act together. But as my journey unfolded, I realized that I'd never loved myself. To be honest, I didn't even like myself. I'd lived small and unseen much of the time and never felt worthy enough to be under any kind of spotlight.

The thoughts of my inadequacy saddened me. I wanted to like and love myself. It was detrimental to my healing and well-being but self-love seemed so foreign and out of my grasp.

Self-love is a difficult concept to explain and learn because it's not something that most of us are taught. Self-love often gets translated as being selfish because we are taught to take care of others even if it requires us to sacrifice our own well-being. We don't want people to view us as vain or inconsiderate because we focus on ourselves.

Because of these misconceptions, it's no wonder that most of us do not understand the concept and the importance of self-love. The realization that I'd always put the needs of others before my own was glaringly clear as the audit of my own life was completed. I'd say that this is common. We play the roles we are handed in life without much thought. Whether it was friends, family members or a romantic relationship, my needs were at the bottom of the priority list. If I was a good person, I'd always help others, or so I thought that was the right thing to do.

Through painful experiences, self-love has become my best ally. It's exactly what I needed to move along my spiritual journey. It's helped me to gain a deep sense of my worth and capabilities.

The idea of having a love affair with myself came rushing to the surface when I spent the holidays alone in New York City right before the breakup with my boyfriend. Dragging my two suitcases and a carry-on bag as I trudged through the snow to a taxi stand at LaGuardia airport was not part of what I envisioned for my Christmas trip to the city. And it definitely didn't feel like a love affair was on the horizon during these tumultuous moments. My bags were heavy and hard to maneuver on the long icy trek in 20-degree weather. I stopped and sat with my bags more than once to have a crying tantrum.

After much struggle, I finally arrived at the shuttle stand after walking about a half a mile, to hop on a bus that would take me to an actual taxi stand since the airport was under major construction. Finally, I was on my way.

Although it may have looked foolish to be traveling with all of this luggage, it has become a part of who I am. It's not just luggage; it's my life.

Admittedly, the love affair with myself began before my arrival in the city. It was just that atmosphere, the energy of the city, and being alone, that brought it to my realization.

When I left Hawaii after being there for three decades, my first stop was in rural New Mexico where I had spent two weeks enjoying visits from local critters and having my friend play a mean tour guide. There was wine on deck as we soaked in majestic mountain views. Self care had begun. My next stops were Florida, Maine and Georgia. Florida and Maine were about reconnecting with family and healing some old wounds. Georgia was the first stop in the next chapter of my life. Each encounter filled me up a bit more. And now, here I was, taking a break from Georgia and in the big city at a magical time of year to take in the city lights.

But this book is not about travel. It's about grief. It's about pain. It's about letting go. But most importantly, it's about learning to fall in love with yourself.

The life that I was experiencing around me was a direct reflection of how I had been taking care of myself. In hindsight, this now serves as a barometer of self-care and self-love. I must admit that focusing inward, taking responsibility and maintaining belief and trust is what led me to fall in love with myself.

During these three weeks, as I explored the city, I thoroughly enjoyed spending time alone. New York City really helped with that. Everyone dines alone so it was easy to sit with and by myself and be mindful of my surroundings and really soak them in and appreciate myself.

Forcing myself to dine in cafes without my phone or a book to distract me was a foreign experience. I mindfully ate and enjoyed my food. As I savored each bite, I soaked in my colorful and lively surroundings. Sometimes I'd chat with others in the restaurants. I never felt alone.

My trips to the museums or just walking around the city gave me a whole new perspective. I didn't need to wait for someone else to enjoy the things that I'd been wanting to do. I was independent and didn't need anyone to help me get around. This was such a liberating thought. I'd begun to feel alive.

One of my spiritual mentors once told me to spend at least 10 minutes alone and in silence each day. He added that "if you can't spend 10 minutes with yourself, what makes you think that anyone else wants to spend time with you?"

Spending this time alone soothed my soul and made me feel more grateful. It allowed me to mend some more of my broken pieces. More importantly, it allowed me to see parts of myself that had gone unnoticed. Qualities that I'd admired in others but didn't realize that I possessed were suddenly apparent. These realizations were a huge gift. When I'd first found out that I'd be spending the holidays alone, I was sad and upset. My ex-boyfriend had lied about having a remote job that he had to do, and I couldn't be accommodated, which left me searching for a place to go for the holidays. In truth, he didn't have to work through the holidays. He actually went to spend a week with his wife and kids. I have no clue what he was doing the other two weeks, but none of that really matters now. Being alone was the best thing that could have happened to me.

I've learned that it's always important to remember to look for the lesson or gift when events unfold in your life. It's not easy to do while you're in the muck of things, but once you can get to that point, you'll have peace of mind and the drive to move on. And not to just move on, but to excel and create the life that you desire and deserve. If things go awry along the way, move through them and keep on trekking.

For me, I've spent some time reflecting on undesirable parts of my life and how these incidents or happenings may have affected me in a positive manner. It doesn't feel good when we are in a difficult situation but if we can heal the hurts and take the gifts, it's a life changer.

For example, being poor while growing up allows me to be more compassionate. My siblings and I lived in the suburbs and went to nice schools. We didn't have the nice clothes and amenities that most other students possessed. It was rough to be different and stand out as a child, especially when trying to hide your differences. Being teased provided me with the gift of tolerance. Not having certain possessions led to unsolicited comments and taunting from other kids at school or in the neighborhood.

Dealing with the challenging teen years with my son gave me the gift of being non-judgmental. Times were tough and overwhelming, but I'm so grateful that he allowed me to see a multitude of perspectives and understand that my parenting skills weren't lacking.

My son has been my most cherished teacher. Children can teach us so much about the world.

I've found that I learn something from everyone that I meet. The gift could be as simple as someone treating you in an unfair manner so that you realize how you deserve to be treated. Everyone has a story, which guides their interactions, and they also have gifts to share with the world.

As I mentioned earlier, most of us are taught from an early age to take care of the needs of others. We are not supposed to focus on ourselves because we will be called selfish or self-centered. More often than not, it's our flaws and faults that are pointed out and the occasional compliments aren't enough to diminish the list of flaws that "need to be fixed."

For some, like myself, that attitude of not being good enough or not measuring up became normal. That voice always seemed to creep in when an accomplishment or goal was trying to be reached just in time to create the resistance and place enough doubt to give up. I've known many intelligent and confident people that let this voice take over. I'd say it's a common occurrence that most people choose not to discuss.

At a young age, conditions are put in place. For example, parents may tell children, "If you get good grades, I'll be proud of you." Comparisons of siblings is another means of diminishing self worth.

Past experiences, mistakes, upbringing and oppressed belief systems all feed the frenzy of self-doubt and instill the absence of self-love. These ingrained beliefs and happenings play over and over in the mind like a broken record. Some of the beliefs may have served you in the past even if only for brief moments, to instill safety or nurture you through a broken-hearted period. But if you don't let them go, it's easy to feel stuck. But remember, you're never really stuck, because you're a decision or thought away from a new and different life or reality.

I'm talking about that feeling you get when you feel like a hamster, running in place on a wheel, and getting nowhere. When these feelings do arise, consider a review of your thoughts and beliefs to see if they are outdated and no longer serve your best interests.

The practice of mindfulness can assist in keeping you present and in the moment. Enjoy what's happening now. Don't dwell in the past or worry about the future. Being in the present moment is the perfect place to be. Think: peace of mind, stress-free, happy and joyful. In that moment, focus on the positive, the beauty, the joy and you'll begin to see that you'll attract more of these things into your life. When we tend to dwell in a space of lack, or worry and anger and upset, more of this is likely to happen.

Sometimes it's easier to live in a state of victimhood than to try and break free. I felt like a victim for much of my life simply from the circumstances that I was forced to endure. Resistance keeps us in place. Doubts, fears of failure, success, and judgment all keep us feeling stuck.

An old saying goes, other people's opinions are none of our business. Heeding this advice is life changing. How people react to us is a reflection of how they feel and not necessarily a barometer of one's worth and what one is able to accomplish. At times, people have said things to me and I knew that they were speaking from their own personal fears and concerns. Other times, people didn't necessarily want me to get ahead. I don't think this is always malicious but maybe a fear that moving into a different arena could possibly leave certain parts and people in your life behind or at least not in the forefront. And there's been times I felt sabotaged because someone was envious of the changes that I was making or the perception of success that was coming my way.

In one instance, a co-worker would offer me high-calories snacks and candy, all the while knowing that I was on a fitness journey. I'd accept them, thinking that she was being nice. A friend who worked with us pointed out that she was trying to sabotage my healthy endeavor efforts but I thought she was crazy. "She's trying to sabotage your diet," she said.

Turns out that she was right. I started paying attention and noticed that this particular co-worker was offering the treats only to me and no one else in the department! It was mind-blowing to think someone would stoop so low to sabotage another person's attempt toward self-improvement.

At the end of the day, none of it really mattered, including her twisted reasoning. A continual focus on self-love helps us to easily move forward with what feels right and true in our lives.

When I look back at the mistakes that I've made, and the heartache that I've endured, I feel a sense of pride. My strength from the lessons that I've learned shines through and reminds me of how I came to find self-love.

So what exactly is self-love?

Simply put, it's a regard for one's own health, well-being and happiness. It sounds easy, right?

For many, it's a foreign concept. It's sometimes challenging for people to know what they need.

What makes you happy? What brings you joy? What do you want to accomplish? These are simple questions that don't always have easy answers. It's a much simpler task to reach out to others and meet their needs.

When asked after my divorce, "What makes you happy?," I was completely dumbfounded and felt blindsided. I started to cry as I pondered how anyone could not know what they like to do and what brings them joy.

Rewind back to my travels and time in New York City. I'd never gone on a solo traveling trip because I had doubted that it would be enjoyable. My thoughts had kept me from enjoying an amazing experience. For each and every day in the city, I'd get up and explore a different area, embarking on long subway rides and seeking adventure. Sitting alone in the cafes and enjoying the sights and sounds was extremely enjoyable. Visiting museums and soaking in the art and beauty didn't require a partner. I learned to love spending time alone and not to settle for less.

I liked myself. Finally! It had taken my entire lifetime up until this point but I'd accomplished this feat that didn't seem feasible. Finally, I could add some things on the list that made me happy. But it didn't stop there. It's been a continual daily practice ever since that most treasured epiphany that I was "good enough" sunk in! I liked and eventually loved myself as days went by, and finding pleasure in simplicity was enticing.

The importance of self-love and self-care cannot be emphasized enough. Learn to make peace with your imperfections. Self-love is critical to one's health and well being. So go and have your own love affair with yourself. You'll be glad that you did. And it's like anything else in life...it's a continual process and practice.

THE SELF-LOVE CHECKLIST

1. The mind is prime real estate. Decide what gets to dwell there.
2. No more comparisons. Only engage in competition with yourself.
3. Create a self-love practice. Start with simple things that provide some peace and joy like sipping a cup of tea, a longer shower or bath with salts or essential oils, or reading a few pages of a good book.
4. Drink more water.
5. Include some sort of movement daily. It could be a simple walk, yoga or stretching, dancing around the house or an intense interval training workout.
6. Nourish the body by eating an array of fruits and vegetables. Make healthy choices but also enjoy some treats. Remember to not feel guilt and shame over choices since those feelings may be more toxic than the treats themselves.
7. Meditate, pray or find some quiet time. Reflection and processing each day allows us to let go of things more easily before they get a deeper hold on us.
8. Practice an attitude of gratitude. It's hard to be angry, sad and fearful when we are focusing on the positive things and giving thanks.

This is my partial list. Make a list of things that will nourish your own soul and deepen your practice of self-love.

CHAPTER 9

THE ART OF LETTING GO

The practice of self-love includes learning to let go of the things that no longer serve you. Letting go sounds like such an easy thing to do, but it's definitely not. If it were easy, everyone would remain in a constant positive emotional state.

We all have childhood hurts or traumas. Those unwanted emotions—whether derived from situations that happened on the playground or during middle and high school years, where feelings of insecurity and inadequacy are a normal part of growing up and becoming who we are as adults—can continue to plague us throughout our lifetime. Few are lucky enough to go through life without adding on relationship conflicts, failures and regrets over the years, all leading to emotional baggage. The negative emotions that we experience have physical consequences because they trigger the body to release toxic chemicals that over the long term can result in physical pain and illness.

In light of traumas, we do our best to shield ourselves from further hurt. Our "shields" are not the physical ones carried by warriors, but mental blocks created in our minds. My shield was my excess body weight. On some level, it made me feel safe. I could blame my weight for holding me back and excusing myself from the hard work of moving myself forward. I didn't have to do anything. My weight guaranteed failure or ridicule if I were to step out of my safe zone, so I thought.

Stuffing my feelings with fast food and unhealthy snacks was normal in the same way that an alcoholic would reach for a drink or a drug addict would seek out a chemical of choice. Food filled the void in my soul and for the brief time I had a plate in front of me or a burger in my hands, the hurt or anger would go away.

Holding on to anger and fears wreaks havoc on the body. I should know. I endured anxiety for decades and it wasn't until I began letting go of things, people, situations and especially emotions that didn't serve me, that those torments began to subside.

I've always lived with my emotions unchecked. I've been deeply sad and I've been deeply angry, which is challenging, but when I'm deeply happy and joyful, I feel as if I'm floating. If you respond to life the same way, the challenge is to find a balance and means to manage your emotions instead of allowing your emotions to control you.

I've had friends who only liked to be around me when I was upbeat and happy. When I was going through darker periods, they expected me to simply "get over it." And I complied for a long time. That stopped once I realized that if I didn't process my emotions and let things go, that the stifled situation would show up later to affect other areas of my life.

Many times I didn't even see the correlation. I've since changed some of those friendship statuses to acquaintances. I realized that some friends weren't able to look at my difficulties because they mirrored their own shortcomings. It's not their fault that they tried to disregard my feelings; if they couldn't handle their own emotions, why on earth would they be able to deal with mine?

Most people don't like to watch others who are hurting and suffering. Although it makes sense, it's important to remember not to live by another person's standards and judgments. It's crucial to work through the muck and not tuck it away for another day. I guarantee that unwanted emotions and situations that are stuffed away will come back full force one day. Hard knocks and lessons may continue to plague you until you've dealt with the problems or issues, found the lessons in them and moved forward.

My lesson has been that if I set aside time to grieve or work through the negative emotions, I'm able to get to a place where healing can begin and forgiveness can happen. Letting go is a catalyst for everyday miracles. There are so many small things that we overlook in our day that are truly miraculous. Just the mere fact that we wake up each day and take more breaths or the way our bodies heal are miracles that we often take for granted. Honoring the simple daily miracles allows us to live in a space of gratitude and love. Then we can be in a space where larger miracles can happen.

It's often fears and judgments that don't let us move forward, and that includes self-judgments. There's a fine line between fear and love, which again instills the importance of self-love. The good news is that love and fear cannot coexist in the same space and neither can peace and fear.

I'm at peace now. When I think about lost love, I can now smile. I'm grateful for the love that I had and continue to have in my life. I've experienced so many wonderful things and had so much spiritual growth because of lost love. It opened doors that provided new opportunities. But that was not always the case. It took a lot of releasing of emotions and letting go, but I did it and so can you.

If you only had a few hours or a day to live, would the baggage that you're carrying around matter? Probably not.

We can choose to act in ways that will either enhance or hinder our personal growth. We can remain stuck in misery or can let go of fear and anguish and move on to better days ahead.

CHAPTER 10

IS IT RESISTANCE?...JUST BREATHE

Just when everything seems to be heading in the right direction, we run out of gas. Those doubts start flooding in. The insecurities return.

Am I worthy of this? I can't do this. Why bother? These are just a few questions and statements that can hinder our growth and success.

Resistance to success comes in many forms but can stop us in our tracks. Emotional struggles from the past often result in internalizing negative messages that we repeatedly replay in our minds, hindering our ability to move forward and achieve our goals.

During these times, it's important to change negative thinking patterns.

Check in and evaluate your mood. Are you feeling like you're not good enough? For much of my life, "not good enough" was a recurring theme. It was ingrained in me from my limiting beliefs or what others said or thought about me. Let me shout it from the rooftops: "You are enough. You're perfect as is!"

Catching these negative thought patterns instilled in us beginning in childhood allows you to take steps to overcome obstacles. These blocks that have been built over time thwart our ability to live the joyful life that we so deserve. Whether it's a fear of failure or a fear of success, remaining in this mindset can lead to hardships, misery, despair or simply that feeling of being stuck. Resistance to change is that defeating force that will keep you feeling that way.

Feeling trapped and stuck is only in the mind. We are always only one thought or action away from living a different life or having a different experience.

Resistance to change has stopped me in my tracks more times than I care to admit. It seems to lurk in the corner and when things are going great, it makes itself known, causing the self doubts to arise. It's definitely stopped me from reaching my goals or pursuing my passions even when success seemed relatively easy.

That larger-than-life force can be overwhelming and debilitating. If you don't nip it in the bud by disregarding the negativity and moving forward with plans or goals, resistance has won. The negative self-talk has prevailed. The "I can't" attitude takes control and steers you down a negative pathway.

Reframing these thoughts has been a huge part of my self-love journey. Thankfully, not feeling good enough has become a thing of the past. I'm not saying that it never happens, but when I find myself wallowing in self-doubt, I'm prepared to go to battle and face it head on. Self-love wins.

If you're willing to embrace self-love, the negative self-talk needs to be shut down. When you're talking to yourself, imagine you are talking to someone that you dearly love, like a little sister or beloved child. We would not talk to another person as harshly as we talk to ourselves. The internal speech is often incessant chatter of past failures, hurts and fears. It's that inner voice that's telling you what's right or what to believe. One way to convert negative thoughts to positive ones is through repetitive affirmations. When you find yourself repeatedly thinking a negative thought, change it to a positive one. For example, I would continually say that my plans never work out or nothing works out for me. I worked hard until I reached a point where I could say with confidence that things always work out for me. It took a long time but the rewards have been many.

By focusing on gratitude and positivity, more of that continues to enter my life. Overall, it's provided a sense of peace. If you're not ready to face any demons, one way to find clarity and peace, even if just for a few moments, is by simply focusing on your breathing. Concentrating on breathing keeps us in the moment and keeps negative thoughts at bay. Breathwork can help one get to a place where they feel ready to move forward.

Deep breathing, meditation, yoga, or just regularly sitting in peaceful and quiet surroundings can have a profound effect on one's well-being. Simply taking the time to breathe can decrease anxiety levels. It's amazing what a few deep breaths can accomplish. When I was condensing my life into a few pieces of luggage, breath work kept me afloat. The breathing exercises kept my anxiety at bay.

Trips to the beach and spending time in nature also helped me to heal after my bad breakup. Just listening to the waves lap the shoreline soothed my soul.

Practicing relaxation techniques on a regular basis helps to reduce stress and anxiety, promote clarity and provide a sense of peace. If you can set up a regular time to establish a routine, even if it's only 5 minutes each day, you'll reap the benefits.

As we rush through life, shallow breathing has become the norm. Deep breathing or simply focusing on the breath can help to anchor us in the present. During moments of stress and anxiety, conscious breathing allows you to shift and release the negative energy instead of storing it in the body. If we don't let go of negative emotions like worry, shame, guilt and anger, the toxic chemicals associated with the body's "flight or fight" response will find a place to be stored in the body, often manifesting in physical ailments, muscle pain, tension, even cancer.

When you focus on the breath and do deep breathing exercises, it sends a message to the mind that it's time to be calm. During some of my darkest moments, my breath was all I had. Fortunately, weekly restorative yoga classes gave me a space where I could let go and just breathe. I could just be without any judgment. The class provided a much-needed weekly reset.

I've been going to the same class for nearly two decades. My teacher has seen me through some pretty tough times. When my mother died, I remember going to class and not even doing one yoga pose. I just lay there in corpse pose, taking breaths and crying for the entire hour. This also happened frequently during my separation and divorce. And, of course, when I returned to the islands after my breakup, my mat provided solace once again. I'm thankful that I learned how to stop and breathe even if I don't practice it all of the time. It's always there to provide a reset when I need it.

Belly breathing is one of the more simple breathing techniques that you can practice. Sit or lie in a comfortable position. Close your eyes, do a couple shoulder shrugs and relax your shoulders. Allow the tension in your body to melt away. Inhale slowly and deeply through the nose. If it helps, place one hand on the belly and one hand on the chest. Exhale slowly from the mouth. You may also consider letting out a heavy sigh. Feel your belly rise as you breathe in. Try committing to this for at least 5 minutes a day. If 5 minutes feels too long, just work on taking more deep breaths throughout the day.

Alternate nostril breathing has also helped me during periods of stress and anxiety. It feels a bit odd at first but it's really beneficial in creating a sense of calm. It involves breathing through one nostril while blocking the other one. For example, place your right thumb over your right nostril. Breathe in through your left nostril. Put your finger over your left nostril and breathe out through the right nostril. Now breathe in through the right nostril and exhale through the left. Continue alternating the breathing pattern until you can get to a point of feeling more relaxed.

Another effective option is equal breathing. It involves timing your breathing so the length of your inhale and exhale are the same. All inhalations and exhalations should be made through the nose. Breathe in for a count of four (or any number that makes you feel comfortable). Hold your breath for a second or two and exhale for a count of four. Repeat the pattern until you start to feel more calm. Personally, the counting causes me more anxiety but we all respond differently, so I'd suggest trying the different options to determine what works best for you.

Everyone deals with stressful situations differently, but these simple breathing techniques will be a powerful addition to your spiritual toolbox.

CHAPTER 11

EVERYONE'S GOT GARBAGE

It's important to have some tools, like breath work, to get through the tough times. No one goes through life unscathed. We've all got junk, or those undesired traits, fears and limiting belief systems that tend to hold us back. Self-comparisons to others amplify any sense of inadequacy.

Some people seem to have their lives completely in order. They walk around with an air of confidence and seem to have an aptitude for happiness. But remember, never judge a book by it's cover. Many of us, myself included, have walked around carrying an abundance of pain, hidden behind a great big smile. We have done work presentations with ease, only to have a breakdown when we are back in the comfort of our homes. I've taken breaks at work to cry in my car during my down days.

One of my friends appeared to have a prim and proper upbringing but in actuality, she had experienced a tumultuous life with young and wild parents. Often left alone or exposed to their partying and arguments, she learned to be quiet and non-confrontational. Not wanting to repeat those patterns, her belief was that one who is boisterous or argumentative was bad. She had gone to the other end of the spectrum to maintain a sense of peace, which didn't always serve her. Putting her own needs aside to create harmony for others didn't leave much room for self-love.

I'm not saying that we shouldn't compromise in our relationships. Some compromise is necessary, but it shouldn't regularly come at a cost that leaves one with a lack of self-love and care.

Keep in mind that self-care doesn't equate to being selfish. The more self-care and attention you provide for yourself, the easier it will be to do more for others. When we are nourished, there's not a feeling of depletion or obligation. We feel good and helping others to feel good seems to come naturally.

So don't think you're one of the unlucky souls carrying baggage, self-inflicted or otherwise, that needs to be released. Everyone has junk that is carried around in invisible backpacks or stored in different areas of their body. Think about this the next time someone complains about a pain in the neck. The physical pain may coincide with their life's circumstances.

Thinking about the junk or trying to get rid of it is easier said than done. Worrying about having to be in a different situation with different struggles can be more stressful than what you're currently dealing with in life. Maintaining familiarity appears easier but it comes at a cost. Many scenarios go on far longer than they should because we don't want to lose our sense of familiarity. Fears continually keep us frozen in place.

Everything that I feared most seemed to happen all at once. And I was still OK. Normally, people's worst fears don't come to fruition but I learned that even if they do, solutions can be found. As I previously mentioned, I'd found myself in a predicament with no place to live, no money, no job, no love relationship and definitely no self-respect. I'd hit rock bottom, not in one area of my life, but in all areas at once. It was a colossal epic fail. I was in a deep ditch, the sort of which there is no hope of climbing out. How does one rise up again when all has been lost?

As a former journalist, I'd talked to people who had experienced similar harrowing life experiences. I could empathize with them and share their stories in order to help others going through traumas. I believe that their stories helped me as I sat in this space, disheartened and at the end of my rope. I didn't feel like I wanted to hold on anymore. I didn't care to muster up the strength that would dig me out of my hole only to land me in another. I had to muster all my strength to take just one step.

Love and faith managed to keep me going as I wallowed in survival mode.

I could see the light at the end of the tunnel but complete darkness took over on more than one occasion. It was very dim and at times not even visible, but I could finally see myself surviving this situation. I could do it. I still didn't know how but the reality that it was possible kept me going. The heartbreak was real but so was the healing. I was OK. I'd always been OK. And you are OK, too. Thoughts and feelings of being OK in spite of everything that happened to me provided a sense of security and eventually monumental confidence. The trek ahead of me was long and daunting but somehow I felt it would be worth the effort.

The process had begun by a shift of mindset, but erasing a lifetime of worry, anxiety and depression would not happen overnight. Worry causes so much physical and mental stress on the body. Worrying, in fact, is much like praying for things to happen just because you've placed so much focus on an issue. If it's something undesirable that you're focusing on, consider shifting your thoughts. It's important to place emphasis on what you want instead of what you don't want.

We all have experiences that don't work or make us feel sad or rejected. We know we don't want to experience the ill feelings again. Doubts and pain can seep in if we allow it, but nobody wants to consciously feel bad.

So take a moment and focus on things that bring you joy and fulfillment. What do they look like?

When doubt starts to drag you down, remember that everyone has junk and keep moving forward. Don't start your day with the broken bits of yesterdays, or worse yesteryears. Each and every day, we are blessed with a brand new beginning. We are given a fresh start. Each day becomes the first day of the rest of our lives. You could even choose to start fresh and shift your thoughts in the next moment or hour; waiting for the next day is not necessary. Why wait? Something wonderful may be on the flipside if you're willing to change your mindset.

Let go of all the rubbish, focus on positive thoughts and believe in yourself. You'll be amazed at what a difference this can make. By doing so, you can shed some of that extra baggage that you've been carrying around.

CHAPTER 12

SHEDDING THE WEIGHT

Speaking of baggage, I dropped 40 pounds in a year, but that's not what I'm talking about here. Sure it was incredible to shed those physical pounds, but I'm referring to the heavy weight that we carry around energetically. Those attachments and anchors that keep us stuck and make it nearly impossible to move forward to achieve our goals or simply be happy.

The process seems simple enough — just let go of unwanted sentiments and memories. But when you've been carrying around hurt and anger like a security blanket, it feels a little odd when it's suddenly missing. My excess weight was like a majestic suit of armor that served as a shield of sorts. The shield was intended to keep pain from entering my space, but as you can imagine, that didn't work out so well for me.

I'd gained weight over the years, with a yo-yo effect of losing and regaining it, but mostly staying on the heavy side. An unhappy marriage, job stress and anxiety provided excuses not to focus on weight loss. I didn't loathe exercise and didn't necessarily indulge in hefty portions of food. I'd written an exercise column as part of my job duties at the daily newspaper and knew exactly how to create and follow a simple and sensible weight loss and fitness plan.

But fears and emotions always managed to sabotage any long term plan of action. For years I had written articles advising people how to take the pounds off or how to find an exercise plan that leads to physical fitness. Unfortunately, there's a certain amount of truth behind the adage, "the shoemaker's son always goes unshod." I could give sound advice, but not practice it myself.

For my entire life, emotional eating provided me with a sense of security whenever I was feeling sad, empty or lonely. It helped, temporarily. Using food to numb my feelings was better than experiencing the full-fledged anxiety, grief or depression.

Foraging for food to ease the pain could be likened to an alcoholic reaching for a drink. You may use the weight as an intentional barrier or the emotional eating may serve as a means to push down any upset. Either way, it's not a healthy way to sort through feelings.

If you tend to eat when you're sad or worried or depressed, it's highly likely that you're stress eating. During times of high stress or life transitions, eating can be a balm. If it becomes a habit, you may find your feeding yourself while in traffic or after you've had a tough day. A daily routine of using food to feel better can become the norm.

After I condensed my life into a few suitcases, not only did I have the excess weight to contend with but I now had situational high blood pressure from an abundance of stress, emotional pain and was generally not feeling well. Emotional eating had been my dear friend for a long time. Sometimes the guilt of overeating was probably more unhealthy than the food I was putting into my body.

One tool that was helpful in breaking my bad habit of emotional eating was pressing the pause button when triggered. If you feel like your hunger is caused by an emotional issue, see if you can wait at least 10 to 20 minutes before reaching for food. Take a few deep breaths and drink some water since dehydration can also be masked as hunger. If you delay eating, and the cravings go away, your emotions were the driving force behind your hunger.

If you continue to practice not being impulsive, it will allow you an opportunity to deal with the issue or emotion that you're trying to suppress. It provides an opportunity for growth.

You'll need to work on being comfortable when you're feeling uncomfortable. I'd always avoided getting to that place of being uncomfortable with my feelings or discomfort in general. I didn't want to focus on the things that would make me feel bad. On a surface level, it seems easier to stuff away those feelings and not give them a second thought. But I've found that these emotions will come rushing to the surface, time and time again, until you work through them, and let them go. Once you've gone through this process, you've taken your power back.

Consider making a list of self-soothing techniques that may help you to keep emotions in check. Writing in a journal, meditation, energy work, creative expression, listening to music, spending time in nature, relaxing baths and essential oils are some of the things on my list. It's important to have some coping tools and to remember that you've got this.

Mindfulness is required when dealing with stress eating. It's amazing how quickly emotions can snowball and make problems appear insurmountable. If you allow an issue to become bigger than yourself, it becomes more frightening, but it doesn't need to stay that way. One of my spiritual mentors regularly reminded me that my problems were not mountains but speed bumps, just a small blip in life, that can be easily maneuvered if one can remain calm.

I was once advised, "Nancy, just stand up; you're in a wading pool and you've got floaties on!"

I'm glad that I was finally able to stand up.

Believe that you can conquer or change the situation even if you need to break it down to small, manageable goals to reach a positive end result. Focus on things other than food, alcohol or other crutch that can relieve stress in a positive way. Believe that once you make a decision, the Universe will open up avenues and conspire to help you meet your goals. And most importantly, remember that the best weight that you'll lose, are the opinions and views of others.

PART 3

YOU'VE GOT THIS!

CHAPTER 13

KNOWING THYSELF

According to legend, "know thyself" is one of the mottos inscribed on the Temple of Apollo at Delphi. It seems fitting because this Greek god is associated with light, healing, oracles and knowledge.

Fortunately, these words of wisdom were also passed down to me by my spiritual mentors. Because we are typically looking for answers outside of ourselves, I'd never given this concept much thought. Once I realized that it's important to look within myself to realize my own power and potential, my life began to shift in a positive manner.

Because so many of us are led to focus outward for much of our lives—taught by our parents, teachers and society to compare ourselves to others to gauge our ranking in the game of life—it may be challenging to get to know our true selves, outside the public arena.

Life flows more smoothly if we understand and acknowledge our physical and psychological strengths, weaknesses, limitations and influences. If we are attuned to these things, we can better control our thoughts, emotions and actions. Self-awareness allows one to see oneself clearly and objectively.

Instead of evading difficult questions when problems arise, stopping to ask and honestly answer questions like, "Why is this happening to me?" or "Why am I so angry?" push us toward a deeper understanding of ourselves. If we truly want to take control of our lives, we must seek out the answers. If we choose to avoid the answers, we tend to get stuck in negative patterns. If you come to know yourself, you'll realize that everything that you need is within you; that you already have all of the answers.

In order to know yourself, continual self-reflection is required. Once you're no longer depending on other people or circumstances, it will be easier to control your destiny. Take the reins and step into your power.

If our emotions were not acknowledged or validated in childhood, it can have a negative effect on us as adults and lead to struggles with self-discipline, self-care, unworthiness issues, disconnection and lack of fulfillment. These issues need to be addressed on a deep level because neglecting emotional states can lead to anger issues, anxiety and depression.

One of my recollections as a young girl was my mom diminishing my need to shed tears. "You'd cry in front of the pope," she said one day.

My response was, "Yes, because he'd help me."

There were other incidents when I felt the "suck it up, buttercup" mantra was more important than addressing an issue. I was taught to be tough and I learned I could handle the adversity and hard knocks. I just didn't realize the long term emotional toll it was taking.

Personal reflection can help you to identify negative patterns, and can help you to stop worrying about things you can't control. You may notice that it's hard to say no or that you continually put yourself in toxic relationships. Do you agree to help or volunteer even though your heart is not into it? Are you looking for love and happiness but instead encountering grief?

I'd say that most of us learn to seek happiness from other people or material things. We are a solution-driven society, so why wouldn't we expect to find the answers this way?

If something happened, I knew I could call half a dozen friends to hash it out and see what I should do. The solution was clearly apparent, but seeking the validation of others seemed necessary. I didn't trust myself to make the right choice. Although the logical solution was right in front of me, if the group didn't confirm this, I'd take their advice only to endure even more pain and then pursue what I knew would be the correct way to handle things before seeking advice.

One would think that after this happened numerous times that it would be much easier to make a decision without others' feedback, and sometimes inevitable heartache. But trusting yourself is difficult after a lifetime of being dependent on others for validation. The truth is that we know better than anyone what we really need. The answers are within us if we are willing to sit quietly and listen for them.

The definition of trust is "to rely upon or place confidence in someone or something." If you're living with doubts and fears and lacking confidence, it would be challenging to trust. The process of letting go of negative patterns will help move you along the path. Setting aside doubts and fears allows trust to start to shine through.

Once you realize that you have all the answers within yourself, the outside search can end. Hallelujah!

By learning to listen and trust the answers within yourself, that wisdom can help you confidently navigate life. Our inner knowing is and has always been there but we need to remember to access it.

We want to feel safe and secure, and because we think that safety comes from outside of ourselves, it's not surprising that we cling to things including success and money, material possessions and even people, when they don't serve us well. We can spend an entire lifetime searching for and chasing after things we feel are missing from our lives. We fail to realize that nothing external will ever bring us the peace and joy that we deserve, because there's nothing more powerful than the voice inside of us. That inner knowing, or gut instinct, will never steer you wrong. Inner wisdom always provides an answer. We just have to take the time to be quiet and listen.

Trust is the first step. Trusting yourself is in itself a process. As you work on building your "letting go" muscles and stacking the self-love and confidence blocks, trust will become more natural and with ease. When you are feeling stuck or unworthy, reframing these thoughts to positive beliefs will help expedite the process.

Contemplating where limiting beliefs came from may be helpful. We are programmed from a very young age by multiple sources including parents, teachers, religion and societal norms. We are taught the "shoulds," "musts" and "must-nots" through both words and actions. The should've, would've, could've syndrome weighs heavily on most of us. Finding the source of the belief may be helpful but it is not necessary to move forward or let go. If something is no longer serving your greatest good, it's time to remove it from the pictures that play in your head. There's always many solutions to any given situation and you, and only you, will know what works best in your life. Contemplate the issue and consider your needs.

When you minimize your own needs, it sets you back a few steps, but perseverance and building strength over time, will keep you on the path. But before you fully trust yourself, you need to know yourself.

Are you happy? Do you feel fulfilled? What triggers negative emotions? What knocks you down? Are you filled with doubts? Are any fears holding you back? Do you need to forgive yourself or anyone else? Once you start asking yourself these questions, you'll most likely realize that there's some blocks and healing to be done.

Most people would claim to know themselves quite well. But then they turn and ask advice from everyone around them. They compare themselves to others. They don't even give themselves a chance. Knowing yourself is much more important than what others know or think that they know about you. An abundance of strength and confidence is gained when we learn to look inward and see ourselves.

Learning to trust your own intuition is critical. Trusting yourself will allow you to grow and flourish.

Here are some tips for trusting your own intuition:

1. Be yourself. It's difficult to trust yourself to make decisions or take actions when you fear the judgments of others.
2. Reframe negative thoughts. When fears and doubts start creeping in, remind yourself that you are powerful, strong, healthy, beautiful; you fill in the adjectives. You've got this and may need to remind yourself regularly.
3. Follow your heart. Listen less to what your brain is telling you. The mind will always play tricks on you. It will work to formulate answers that may not serve your highest good. Learn to listen with your heart.
4. Find your tribe. Surround yourself with folks who want to see you succeed and act as cheerleaders. They will encourage you to trust your instincts and follow your dreams.
5. Let things go. Yes, it's a repetitive theme because doubts and fears cloud intuition and make it harder to trust yourself.
6. Always speak kindly to yourself. Believe your own words. Know the power of the spoken word and choose words wisely. Words have the ability to help or harm us; to uplift us or administer defeat.
7. Everyone makes mistakes so when you get knocked down, get back up and start again. Just because something didn't turn out as planned, don't allow that to lead you to doubt your intuition in other circumstances.

Once you begin to trust your intuition, the real magic happens.

CHAPTER 14

THE ART OF FORGIVENESS

It's challenging to trust your intuition if you're hanging onto a bunch of grievances. Forgiveness is necessary for the healing process. Forgiveness comes in different forms but it's always to benefit oneself. Often we may not feel that someone deserves our forgiveness but if we hold onto the pain, hurt and anger, we are only hurting ourselves.

Buddhist teachings share that holding onto anger is like grasping a hot coal. The intention is to throw it at the other person but in the end, you only end up burning yourself.

Forgiveness can help you break free from the control of the person who wronged you. It allows you to take back your power. It doesn't mean that you forget about or dismiss or condone the actions. It's more about finding a way to move forward in a peaceful manner.

Being hurt by someone that you trust raises an array of emotions from anger and hurt to grief and depression. It's easy to be consumed by those feelings, making it nearly impossible to move on and enjoy everyday life again. Some of the benefits of forgiveness include feelings of peace, joy, happiness, an increased sense of self-esteem and confidence, and a deeper sense of understanding and compassion.

Just stopping the repeating story of injustice that plays in your head will increase your feeling of well-being. When we choose to forgive someone we aren't letting them off the hook or saying that what they did was OK. It doesn't mean that the pain you experienced will immediately disappear. We still need to make peace with what's happened to us and finding that peace eventually makes the process worthwhile.

Forgiveness provides a release of the anger, pain and resentment. Anger and resentment can linger for years even after we claim to have gotten past a painful situation. In order to release resentment, take some time to sit with the pain. Consider reasons why the person who wronged you may have committed his or her actions. It's often due to some sort of fault or failing in their personality, upbringing or life experiences. In my case, I learned the hard way that my ex-boyfriend was a broken man. He was a liar. He couldn't help himself as he roamed around causing pain for multiple women as he tried to fill a void that none of us could fill.

Am I making excuses for his horrendous behavior? Of course not. But if I failed to forgive him and move on I'd be stuck with carrying more baggage into future relations and situations. So I made the choice to be compassionate toward myself.

One of my spiritual mentors once told me that I carried around an invisible backpack that was filled with problems, a heavy load of problems that were not even my own. I'd continue to gather problems and add them to the mix. This mentor simply asked me, "Why don't you just take off the backpack and give the problems back to who they belong to?"

So that's exactly what I began to do. Slowly but surely, I started to return the problems and worries to their rightful owners and what a relief that provided. I literally understood what people meant when they referred to carrying the weight of the world on your shoulders. I was carrying the heavy load on my shoulders and my back. There's such a freedom in releasing things that don't belong to you. By doing so, we can take back our personal power.

But in the beginning, the betrayal I felt from my boyfriend's actions seemed unforgivable. The idea that he watched me uproot my entire life—when it obviously wouldn't work out long term with all of the relationships that he was juggling—was unfathomable. The unbearable pain of loss on so many levels overwhelmed me as I wondered how he'd allowed me to give up all that was familiar for a relationship he likely had no intention of making permanent. It took months, which felt like years, to resurface from the bottomless pit I felt like I'd fallen into in the aftermath. My mind knew that it was necessary to let go and forgive, but my heart wasn't ready. I knew that holding onto the pain, hate and anger would only hurt me in the long run, but forgiving wasn't easy.

It took lots of prayers and support from family and friends just to initiate the letting go process. But once I forgave the parties involved, my healing began and I continued to peel away the layers of hurt.

Nearly a year after my breakup, I found myself feeling out of sorts. After some contemplation, I realized that the anniversary dates surrounding the start of my ordeals were around the corner. I'd thought that I'd gotten past the whole incident but I came to a realization that recalling my heartbreak had me feeling shattered all over again. Forgiving myself was to be yet another step in the healing process.

Self-forgiveness may be the hardest form of forgiveness to tackle. Sometimes you don't even realize that it needs to be done. But once it surfaces, it's harder than being angry or hurt by others since we tend to be harder on ourselves. The words or actions we direct toward ourselves don't always match advice you'd give another person in the same situation. Again, self-love will save the day. Learning to kick the habit of negative self talk is critical. It's absolutely necessary to forgive yourself for any past actions, lack of action or personal wrongdoings if you want to shed the heavy burdens and find more joy in life.

Imagine talking to a dear friend, a child or even a stranger. You most likely would not talk as harshly to them as you do to yourself. Think about someone who you'd greet with extreme kindness if they were suffering in any way, and replace any negativity you feel toward yourself with that positive verbiage. Imagine how different it would feel if you treated yourself with such kindness.

Acknowledge and take responsibility for your own mistakes and wrongdoings that may have contributed to a bad situation, but don't dwell in feelings of guilt and shame.

Take some time to consider whether forgiveness is needed in some area of your life. Make a list of everyone that you need to forgive. It doesn't mean that you need to talk to the person again if that's not in your best interest, but it may help to put the information down on paper to start releasing some of the negative feelings that you've been harboring. You may become aware of the ease at which your feelings flow from pen to paper.

Next, writing forgiveness letters—even if you never send them—allows for a clear expression of feelings regarding your grievances, and doesn't require contact with the person who hurt you. Letter writing provides a safe means to get your feelings out without the worry of judgment or being hurt again.

I've never sent forgiveness letters I've written. The letters were always intended to be seen by my eyes only. One-sided conversations and letters have worked well for me when dealing with someone who has died. It gave me closure to any unfinished business. One example would be the death of my biological father. He left my family when I was 4 and didn't choose to maintain a relationship with me. Abandonment issues plagued me throughout my life because of this circumstance. Writing a letter that expressed my hurts and pains helped me to move forward and forgive him.

These letters can allow a sense of control over a situation over which you feel helpless. It's all about severing any remaining negative connections so that you can leave that person in your past and not look back. Once the letters are written or printed if you decide to type them, be sure to dispose of them as a means of letting go.

Burning the letters can provide a cathartic healing experience. There's something powerful about watching those painful words melt and turn into ash. If you don't have a safe space to burn the letters, shredding or burying them as a means of disposal works too.

When writing the letters, self-forgiveness often comes into play. At least that was my experience as I embarked on this exercise. It may have to do with the person or situation or reflect how it affected my emotions or how I allowed bad circumstances to rule my life.

Forgiveness letters, delivered or destroyed, whether written to yourself or others, can describe in detail how you felt and the hurt, pain, betrayal and frustration you endured. Be sure to express that you've made a conscious choice to let it go. Forgive the other person. This act ensures that the person or situation no longer has a hold on you. You've taken your power back. It removes the painful burdens and negative emotions.

Any means of finding forgiveness will set you free.

Spending decades in Hawaii, I was fortunate that one of my spiritual mentors introduced me to the Hawaiian forgiveness practice Ho'oponopono. The practice that I learned was not the traditional practice but the modern day version founded by Morrnah Simeona, a healer who was named a Living Treasure of Hawaii in 1983. She was invited to present Ho'oponopono to the United Nations in New York City and the World Health Organization. Dr. Ihaleakala Hew Len later used these techniques to cure an entire ward of patients at a state hospital in Hawaii. The patients were deemed criminally insane, and without ever seeing a patient, he used this practice to heal the patients by focusing on what needed to be healed within himself, which in turn helped the patients to heal.

This practice is both simple and profound. Reciting the phrases with intention, "I'm sorry," "please forgive me," "thank you" and "I love you" was life changing for me. The phrases can be repeated in any order. When I did this practice not only did things shift positively for me but for others around me.

The idea is that we are all interconnected. We are responsible for all of the thoughts in our mind. We tend to view things outside of ourselves as not being our responsibility. But in reality, we are responsible for everything that enters the mind and is brought to our attention. Along with this harsh reality comes this beautiful forgiveness practice that allows you to help facilitate the clearing and cleaning of the negative situation, thoughts or emotions for all of those that are involved.

When I practice this, I ask for forgiveness for any role that I played in a given situation. For example, I typically ask a question like, "What is it in me that is causing (person's name) to have anxiety," and then I repeat the phrases over and over. This has been an extremely helpful healing tool for me to clear energy from both past and current situations. This practice was a gift and blessing during some of my darkest days. If this sort of practice resonates with you, I'd say, it's definitely worth a try.

It doesn't really matter what avenue you choose to take, just be sure to make forgiveness a priority so that you stop giving your power away.

CHAPTER 15

STOP SLEEPWALKING THROUGH LIFE

If you've ever been in a rut it's relatively easy to understand the sleepwalking through life concept. It's that feeling of living on auto-pilot, causing every day to blend into the next, each with a lack of purpose. The same thoughts and activities run through your mind as you wander about unaware and unconscious of your purpose and the impact of decisions you have made. You've decided that life is happening to you, and not for you. If you are in this state, chances are that you'll repeat negative relationship patterns and stay stuck in a mindset that prevents you from attaining the life that you desire. If you're stuck in this state, it's time to stop the negative self-talk and chatter in your head, take control and start living again.

I was stuck on a survival mode setting but once I realized this and awoke, my life began to shift.

At some point, I realized that I had been sleepwalking through much of my life. I was operating in zombie mode, unaware of who I was or my place in the world. Turbulent memories of childhood, remaining in unhealthy relationships longer than I should have and working at dead-end jobs helped to affirm this state of being. Normally, it would take a crisis to shake me up long enough to respond, but once it passed I would eventually revert back to being on auto-pilot and feeling numb.

The breaking point of my marriage was one of those events that woke me up. At that time, I experienced a Britney Spears-style meltdown at a family reunion in Florida. During my travels I got sick, was diagnosed with pneumonia and ended up staying home while everyone was enjoying an array of planned activities.

My ex-husband and I had been fighting constantly long before the trip. He made sure to take our son to the places that he knew were on my "must do" list when I was too sick to go. Between the illness and the tension, I just couldn't manage my emotions anymore. I had a mental breakdown and my siblings blamed me for ruining the trip, especially my brother and his husband. It was my brother who encouraged me to invite my now ex-husband in the first place because, he reasoned, it might "make things better" in my marriage. I suppose I knew it was a bad idea but did it anyway. Ugly crying and screaming fits led to puking.

My frazzled state had everyone on edge. My siblings retreated like turtles hiding in their shells and I knew I was on my own, which left me feeling completely abandoned in my darkest hour. My actions may have been irrational but my anger was deep-seated and they couldn't see my acute pain through the charade I had been living for years. There were lots of demands on my part, and everyone suffered. It was an absolutely horrible trip. My siblings didn't talk to me for many months after this gathering.

"I'd ruined the trip and made everyone miserable," they concurred. It was true but I needed them. This scenario led to more self-awareness but it also rekindled my fantasy of being a princess switched at birth. After all, how could I be in a family with these people who didn't even care about my pain? I deserved much better than that.

My siblings definitely didn't understand the depth of my despair or realize that my marriage was irreparable. They couldn't see that I was completely downtrodden. But I suppose in hindsight, how could they? I'd shared tidbits of my life but those who haven't lived through similar events would find it hard to comprehend.

When you go through a separation or divorce, a multitude of emotions arise. You can feel devastated one minute, liberated the next, and those feelings can switch frequently, leaving one feeling angry, lonely or hurt.

In hindsight, I'm grateful for my breakdown. It woke me up long enough to make a different and difficult decision that allowed me to move forward.

At that time, my mood swings ranged from being happy one moment to sobbing the next. The emotional roller coaster ride left me in a constant state of heightened anxiety. I was smiling on the outside and crying on the inside.

Ending a marriage or a longtime relationship is never an easy choice but it can be one of the most empowering events in life since we tend to experience growth in the aftermath of pain.

Time helps to heal a broken heart and love can be found again. You just need to be willing to take responsibility for your life and happiness. Sometimes our goals and dreams fall by the wayside in pursuit of goals that meet the expectations of others. When this happens, we can go into a deeper state of sleepwalking. For some folks, it may be easier to convince yourself that the life you have is the best that life can be, even when it isn't the case. It makes sense that people have midlife crises. It's a period when we are wise enough to finally wake up and realize that we simply aren't living life.

Sleepwalkers are passive when it comes to dealing with life happenings. Control has been handed over to others. It's easy to become insensitive to the reactive state that we live in and become unaware of how we respond to our surroundings and daily events. The day may be filled with activities that create distractions, such as excessive shopping, overeating, surfing the net or watching television.

Awareness is key to breaking the habit of sleepwalking through life. Once you have gained awareness of the problem, there's no turning back. You'll no longer dread getting out of bed in the morning, other people's emotions and feelings won't have such a profound affect on you and letting go of limiting belief patterns will become easier. You won't need to be burdened by beliefs that have been holding you back or keeping you feeling stuck. You'll know that you're enough; and that you've always been enough. So don't waste any more precious time.

Open your eyes, open your heart and let go of all of the things that no longer serve you. Stop sleepwalking through life and start living life to the fullest.

CHAPTER 16

FINDING YOUR CENTER

So you've got forgiveness down, but you're still not feeling quite right. Feeling off balance and out of sorts can lead us to go off and cry in a corner or lash out at others. Finding your spiritual center can alleviate these types of stresses. Find your center and you'll find inner strength. Focus on the present moment to feel grounded and find stability. Centering involves using your mind to redirect energy to the center of your body, resulting in a sense of inner calm. The spiritual center is a place within yourself where you can find peace even if only temporarily. Mental, emotional and physical peace can be found in this space.

For me, finding my center literally meant finding God. I needed to find and maintain that connection. I'll emphasize once more that it's important to find another label if the idea of God doesn't resonate with you or stops you from moving forward. Some refer to this as source, the universe, the sun, the moon, Mother Earth; others would refer to their higher self. One friend finds centeredness through K-pop. It's all good as long as it keeps you connected to a higher power that you recognize and understand. If you are not religious, viewing spirituality as how one exists and connects with the people in their life and how one fits into the grand scheme of the universe makes it easier to understand how we are all interconnected. Once we become disconnected from source, we may feel confused or poorly about ourselves.

I was mad at God for a long time, probably off and on for my entire life, which often left me feeling disconnected and angry at the world. That's a long time to be mad. That way of thinking kept me angry at myself and it's really hard to be happy when you're angry at yourself. That's when that "not good enough" attitude creeps in, making it impossible to find a healthy dose of self-confidence and self-esteem. So can you see where the spiral is headed in these types of circumstances?

If you don't feel good about yourself and you're filled with doubts and fears, it's highly unlikely that you will be able to meet your life's goals, even a goal as simple as finding joy in simple things.

We may feel like we are not enough and insecurities get the better of us. Am I smart enough? Pretty enough? Many of these issues arise when we start comparing ourselves to others. When we do this, self-love gets tossed out the window. Our self-worth is diminished when we feel we can't measure up to others' successes.

The only person you should be competing with is yourself. Many children grow up with parents, teachers, family members or peers telling them that they are not good enough. Some are treated as if they are worthless and others may have been held to unrealistic standards. Others may have had helicopter moms and were not allowed to make their own decisions. In adulthood, this can be challenging since you're always looking outside for help and answers. Even if we can make decisions, looking for happiness outside of ourselves is the norm. Most of us don't learn the importance of looking inward and finding connection.

Once I began to focus inward and stopped searching outside of myself, things took a positive turn. I took the time to connect to my inner voice, which allowed me to have clarity about the simple things that matter to me. The realization that my purpose was simply to find joy and be the best version of myself became apparent.

I've found different ways to reconnect to source when I'm feeling off course. The first step is to become aware that you're feeling off balance. For me, a dip in the ocean or a stroll in nature can provide an instant reset. When I have time, yoga and meditation does the trick. Just a few minutes of quiet reflection time can make a huge difference. Creative outlets can help you get centered. Elevate yourself by immersing yourself in imagination and the art of creation.

If prayer or talking to angels or guides brings you comfort, try those things to find connection. Regular prayer and meditation are an integral part of my day to help me along my path. I'm always talking to God and angels and have learned that this sort of support system will never let me down.

Grounding in general is important, so if it's easier to imagine yourself having roots that connect into the earth, like a strong majestic tree, go that route. Daily grounding visualizations or meditations can be helpful. Walking barefoot in the grass or on the beach provides an instant sense of grounding for myself. Nature has helped me to weather many storms in my life.

It doesn't matter what tool you use. My belief is that there are thousands of possible ways to reach a destination. Finding the one that will help you on your path is the more challenging aspect.

I'd suggest trying all different ways until you figure out what soothes your soul and brings that sense of peace and connectedness. I'm confident if you do a bit of searching that you'll find some new tools that can be stored away for when they are needed.

When you are living in the here and now, you're focused on what's going on around you. None of us are promised a tomorrow, so the present moment is all we have. Be clear on your intentions and plant seeds for the future but remember to remain rooted in the present moment. If you're centered, grounded and focused on what's happening moment by moment, you'll alleviate anxiety about the future or regrets or sadness from dwelling in the past.

CHAPTER 17

LURKING IN THE SHADOWS

The way that we view ourselves is extremely important. Accepting all parts of ourselves is challenging if we view ourselves in a negative light. Self-criticism can make it nearly impossible to stay centered or get ahead in life. Although educators and psychologists often talk about the power of positive reinforcement and praise, unfortunately, too few of us grow up in positive environments. As a result, many of us eventually adopt negative core beliefs such as not being good enough, smart enough or attractive enough. These crushing beliefs can prevent us from trying to move forward, which means that goals become elusive and unattainable.

Our self-identity strongly affects our daily well-being. Even though we have the power to change our values and beliefs over time as we experience life and broaden our viewpoints, we often hide our true selves and suppress our needs in an effort to please others. If there is a large gap between our inner and outer identities, daily life becomes exhausting. Yet, most of us muddle through life wearing an array of false masks.

When I first began to delve into a deeper level of spirituality, focusing on love and light appeared to be the simple answer for my problems. I thought that keeping darkness at bay helped me to stay in a higher space or vibration. Although that's a true statement, I could not be fully in a conscious state without accepting my dark and undesirable traits lurking in the shadows.

A review of these darker and undesirable feelings—rage, anger, shame, sadness, grief, embarrassment and guilt—often referred to as shadow work, is a game changer. Shadow work is the conscious effort of exploring the dark feelings that bring up the shame, embarrassment and fear within yourself. Many of these undesirable feelings reside in the subconscious and arise when we are triggered by life experiences.

We all have darker aspects of ourselves that remain in the shadows as a means of helping us to avoid pain. Since none of us can truly escape pain over the long haul, the exploration of the true self is challenging but worthwhile. If you're not willing to explore those areas, you'll continue to wear different masks through life and live by other people's standards and expectations, and that's no fun.

We all have negative, deeply ingrained patterns that often start in childhood. Nobody wants to admit that they have bad traits, but finding balance between the light and dark areas is crucial. When we are able to find harmony by making friends with our inner demons, we can embrace both our positive and negative traits, which allows us to maintain a healthy personality. Self-exploration always results in a deeper sense of awareness.

Misery was a constant presence I encountered simply because, as a people pleaser, I cared that people liked me. The opinions of others were more important than how I viewed or understood myself. I sacrificed my values to make others happy, which only caused more darkness hidden deep inside of me to surface.

When I dove into shadow work, it wasn't intentional. Things had ended so abruptly in my relationship that I was left with no sense of direction and had lost all hope. I was completely and utterly lost. I'd bottomed out and felt alone and felt life was meaningless. It was extremely difficult to go through the basic motions of life so I didn't have much energy to worry about others' opinions.

I spent many days and nights crying, lying in a fetal position, and contemplating whether it was worth it to keep on living. The horrible feelings of helplessness and hopelessness forced me to take a hard look at what had transpired in my life. Radical honesty was required. Lying to myself about how I felt or telling myself how I should feel was no longer an option. My life needed a complete review and overhaul. Not only did I relive the hurt of the breakup but also other areas of my life that had remained unhealed. The areas of my life that were unfulfilled because of fears or insecurities and a lack of confidence.

Feeling stuck in the muck is not fun, but after going through this and getting to the other side, I feel that the process was worth the pain. I'd managed to remove the masks and be myself after a painful shedding of previous structures that I'd created and built in my life. I'd experienced a spiritual crisis, which made perfect sense because I'd lost everything—my identity, stability, relationship and career. All of the belief systems that I'd been carrying were shattered along with my hopes, dreams and sense of trust.

The pain that I was feeling allowed for personal development. The major transitions allowed me to reach a deeper perception of life and viewpoint of how I fit into the grander scheme of things. I began to love myself completely and it allows me to love others in their completeness.

We can take inventory of our self-identity, which comprises personality, skills, physical attributes, knowledge and abilities. Shadow work helps us to recognize the dark side of our personality, and is an ideal means to heal the wounded self.

The word "persona," conceived by Swiss psychiatrist Carl Jung, describes the mask that each of us wears to hide our deep self from the world around us. Any aspect of ourselves that is not exposed to the light of our consciousness fits into this category. According to Jung, the disowned parts of our personalities that the ego fails to acknowledge and accept, become the hidden side of our psyche, which I refer to as the shadow.

The shadow most often surfaces in our judgment of others or as a mirror in our relationships. For example, a person in a bad relationship can choose to blame their partner for treating them poorly, but chances are both partners play a part in unhealthy scenarios. Finding the shadow aspects of yourself requires being critical of your own behaviors. Are you passive or aggressive? Do you have issues with anger, jealousy or selfishness?

These dark traits of the self typically run deep since they are created by our earliest experiences with relationships. They are continually reinforced by culture and social norms.

My issues and fears of abandonment began early on. As a young child, I recall wondering why my father didn't come home so that we could have a normal family. The abandonment theme repeated throughout my life, especially when it came to men as I'd find myself in relationships where my partner was emotionally unavailable. I found myself giving too much and hiding my fears in hopes that abandonment would not occur.

When situations and arguments happened with friends or even my siblings, the abandonment issues could creep in and wreak havoc on my psyche. I'd just maintain composure and try to smooth everything out to avoid the possibility of ending up alone. I built strong walls and barriers to protect myself from pain and heartache.

In order to embrace and accept the darkness within, we need to break down all of the walls and barriers that we have built to protect ourselves.

For instance, I didn't want my broken heart to be wounded again, so I needed to allow love in. I needed to love myself, all of me, including the darkest parts. It was terrifying to feel whole again because that was setting me up for an opportunity to feel emptiness, which was inconceivable.

When I dealt with the breakup, I entered an unfamiliar dark space. It was scary as anger, rage, fears, shame, guilt and an array of undesirable emotions came rushing to the surface. A couple of my friends' judgments made me feel worse as I continued to wallow. My belief is that they just wanted me to stop being so dark and ugly, and rightfully so. But it was wallowing in the darkness that brought me to light and transformation. It allowed me to stand up and be myself without the worries and judgments of others.

When I finally did come back, I evolved into a different person. The darkness became a part of who I am and the integration helped me to find a deep sense of self-love.

Fragments of what makes us who we are often become lost in the shadows, leaving us with feelings of emptiness, so I needed to make a conscious effort to explore these long-ignored feelings. My belief is that you need to feel it to heal it. In order to be healed and feel whole, you must embrace and integrate both the light and the dark aspects of yourself.

The more that you try to suppress your true self, which includes your shadow side, the more it will come out in destructive and self-sabotaging ways.

It's also important to be aware of what triggers you about other people's behavior when you're doing shadow work. If anger erupts or sadness and grief, you may be recognizing your own deficiencies in others. When we pay attention to what irritates us about others, we can gain a better understanding of ourselves. Be mindful if you're drawn to something when it's not in your best interest. Hiding in the shadows can lead you on a path of people-pleasing and mask-wearing instead of being your true self.

In order to be authentic and come into our power, we must fully know ourselves. Negative qualities must be accepted. Jung viewed this process as encompassing the philosophical, mystical, and spiritual aspects of being human.

Learning to accept ourselves without judgments is critical to our well-being. Ignoring the shadow self takes a great deal of effort and energy. Creativity can be depleted or dampened in the process. Stress and anxiety or even depression can take control. When you're able to accept all aspects of yourself—the good, the bad and the ugly—it's much easier to compose positive ideas or become more creative and imaginative.

Playing with the ideas of self-identity and shadow work can provide inner strength and a greater sense of balance, which allows one to be better equipped to take on life's challenges. Shadow work is the process of acknowledging and accepting the hidden parts of your personality.

By acknowledging and accepting our weaknesses and shadow side, the results are fruitful. Not only will you be able to work on eliminating destructive behaviors, but you'll have a clearer perception of who you really are, which results in better relationships.

It can help improve communication and get out of the mindset that things are out of reach. Accepting all parts of myself has allowed me to forgo the excuses and cop-outs that I'd entertain that kept me from following my dreams. It's never too late to pursue our dreams and goals. Using unfulfilled dreams and desires to transform your life can be extremely liberating. Accepting ourselves completely lets us escape victimhood.

Stop allowing others to control your happiness. Embrace your dark side and move into the light. This is heavy work, so remember to be patient, provide yourself some grace and compassion as you explore and confront your shadow side. It may not seem worthwhile when you're on the downside, but trust me, once you get to truly be yourself, you'll wonder why you waited so long to explore the darkness as you remained lurking in the shadows. People may not like you or may not be as accepting once you remove your masks. In hindsight, you'll be happy that they stepped aside. Those who can't accept you completely don't deserve a space in your tribe.

CHAPTER 18

THE PATH OF LEAST RESISTANCE

Before embarking on deeper spiritual work, I ignored lots of painful things about my life. Taking the path of least resistance meant that I always opted for the easy way out of problems. Following the path ensured that all my basic needs would be met, whether I was happy or not. I had been familiar with being in survival mode since childhood. Fears of not having enough and fears of not being enough continually plagued my thoughts and kept me in place. I kept myself hidden much of the time. I didn't take risks and I definitely did not pursue any goals that might reaffirm my "not good enough" status. And why would I?

After exploring and accepting the darker aspects of myself, I now look at the path of least resistance, not as following the easiest path, but following my choice of path without force. No force is needed to reach a goal. I've come to adopt an attitude of acceptance and allowing myself to go with the flow of life. This makes everything so much easier. Surrendering to the path of least resistance allows us to let go of justifications. Once a direction is determined, and the necessary action steps can be taken, I've found that I can achieve the things that I want without stress and pressure, which in the past would have been unimaginable.

Subconscious and deep-seated beliefs cause the need to worry and push with force. The fears that you can't reach a goal or move to the next step make their way to the surface if you are feeling "not good enough" or don't have faith, trust and belief in the process.

Let me remind you that you're much stronger than you think. As time passes, and you're able to stop dwelling in emotions, wallowing becomes a thing of the past. Congratulations; letting go has triumphed.

You're perfect as is and it's a matter of seeing that for yourself. We go through life being evaluated in all areas. In school, we are graded, and see where we measure up to our fellow students. The scores on a piece of paper determine our worth from a very early age. We are constantly shown the things that need improvement. It's an ongoing battle to fix ourselves. Self-improvement is needed constantly if we want to succeed in this world, or at least that's what we learn. Later, we go to jobs where we are regularly evaluated and our weaknesses are pointed out. There's always room to grow, but it's hard to flourish when you're feeling negatively critiqued. On top of all of the typical societal norms, in both religion and culture, we learn to feel bad about ourselves for not doing things a specific way.

My point is that we are repeatedly told from the start that we just "aren't good enough," but with some schooling and lots of effort, we can become a better person. We can meet those standards and excel. Sadly for some folks, they get stuck in this paradigm and it's never enough.

Stop beating yourself up for any shortcomings that may be swirling around in your mind. One big step that helped the most was when I stopped comparing myself to others. I stopped caring about what others were accomplishing. I stopped making a review list in my head of the things that I wasn't accomplishing and they were despite my giving my all to projects. Resigning oneself to feeling unworthy is a slow death sentence that won't lead you down a path of joy or wellness. If you find yourself angry about someone else's success or dwelling on the bad hand that you were dealt, you're only robbing yourself of peace. Dwelling on inadequacies simply elicits regret and mourning. Depending on your programming, you may be ashamed by your lack of success.

My "lack of" attitude began at a young age. My family lived in the suburbs in a middle class neighborhood growing up, but we were poor. I'd go to a friend's house for a slumber party and felt like I was in a castle. I had a big family, so by the time my mother had bought each of us the basic necessities, such as food and clothing; an outfit, jackets, undergarments, boots and shoes, there were no funds for extras. I started working at 14 so that I could buy things my parents couldn't afford. I learned how to wear a mask and fit in.

Start thinking about what causes any feelings of inadequacy you may have. Instead of beating yourself up, consider letting the belief or feeling go. If you're not quite ready for that, try to reframe your thoughts, if only temporarily, and focus on the positive aspects in your life. When we focus on gratitude, it's hard to continue feeling bad.

Some people feel that if they do not focus on their shortcomings, it will cause them to be complacent or lazy and will not allow them to get ahead. But comparison of peers will only bring harsh judgments on yourself and others. The judgments won't help you to perform better and in some cases may diminish your goals. The only person that you should be in competition with is yourself. If you want to strive to be better or do something more efficiently, it's easy to compare it to your last attempt. It's wonderful if you're trying to perfect skills or excel in a specific area. My point is not to carry around a bag of guilt, shame, jealousy and a gamut of emotions that will hurt you and keep you stuck as you get immersed in the "not good enough" arena. Move on. Believe in yourself. You deserve it.

As you practice these skills, you'll gain more emotional intelligence, which is discussed in the next chapter. When we are doing things for the right reason, and are aligned with our goals, things tend to flow naturally and easily. If I'd started beating myself up for the chain of events that occurred after condensing my life into a few pieces of luggage, I wouldn't be experiencing the miraculous wonders of life. Find your own path and embrace the magic.

PART 4

THE MAINTENANCE PLAN

CHAPTER 19

WORKING THROUGH EMOTIONS

Emotions often get in the way as we move through the journey of life. There's a gamut of emotions that can lead us astray and away from self-love but the ones that stand out are anger and resentment, grief and sadness, shame and guilt and loneliness. The list could go on and on. But all of these secondary emotions come from a place of fear or love.

A secondary emotion is a reaction to one's thoughts, such as feeling depressed over your reaction in a situation. It works as a shield that deflects uncomfortable primary emotions so they can be avoided or kept at bay.

Love and fear are the foundation of all emotions. If we can learn to view our feelings under these two categories, it can make it easier to control our emotions instead of our emotions controlling us.

Love is a feeling of well-being that evokes positive emotions. Happiness, peace, contentment, empathy and joy flow easily when you're in a space of love.

When fear creeps in, anxiety, worry and dishonesty may be prevalent. We may feel hopeless or depressed.

When you become more aware of your own emotions, it's easier to take action to move back into a space of love and peace.

Anger and Resentment

Anger can be a natural and healthy response to situations. More often than not, it's a disruption of the present moment and how we had perceived things to be. If we hold on to anger too long, resentments are inevitable.

Anger is a secondary emotion that may come from jealousy, embarrassment, hurt or disappointment. Anger may also be a mask for sadness and grief.

When my friend's husband died suddenly at a young age, leaving her to raise three kids on her own, she went through all of these emotions.

"I didn't sign up for this," she said. She was angry about being left alone but her true feelings were a profound sense of loss and grief. Her sadness was overwhelming. After the initial anger, she was able to let the tears flow and work through the emotions of grief.

Resentment is similar to anger but emanates from negative feelings caused from past experiences. Resentment causes us to continually revisit the experience of past injustices, whether they are real or they're just perceived. Some people hold resentments for decades or entire lifetimes as they keep replaying stories of mistreatment in their head. Even if the initial anger subsides, the resentment still sits dormant, waiting for a trigger. Both of these negative emotions, when held in the body, can end in physical pain or ailments, so it's important to figure out how to process these feelings.

Physical exertion may help to release feelings of anger. Try hitting a punching bag, taking a run or engaging in any form of exercise, as it may help to release some pent-up emotions. Relaxation may work better in some situations. Breathing, meditation, yoga or simply finding something positive to focus on can create a calm state of mind. Journaling is another consideration for releasing emotions.

If you can't find a way to release heavy emotions, seek out a counselor or trusted friend with whom you can share your feelings and work through the process. You have to feel the emotions if you want to heal the emotions.

Sadness and Grief

Sadness is a strong attribute of grief. Both sadness and grief leave us feeling weighed down.

These emotions are inevitable in our lives. We lose loved ones through death or other means. We experience heartache and loss. We watch the sad affairs and suffering of the world.

These emotions can be all consuming and keep you in the dark. Not dealing with the pain only creates more suffering.

Unfortunately, the sorrow must be felt and acknowledged before it can be released. If sadness and grief are ignored, it could lead to more challenging conditions such as depression and anxiety.

Although crying can be attributed to weakness, I'd prefer to view it as a sign of strength that you're willing to work through strong and heavy emotions. People who tamp these feelings down aren't strong enough to deal with the repercussions of sitting with the pain. This one really resonates with me. It's the reason that I carried so much excess weight on my body, which acted as a makeshift protective shield that prevented more pain from entering my space. Once the floodgates opened, not only was I able to work through the emotions but I was able to drop physical pounds, too.

A good cry can do wonders. After the weeping subsides, healing can begin as crying provides a physical means to move the emotion out of the body. It's as if these tears are removing the negative emotions from the depths of your soul. Tears allow the body to release stress and a gamut of negative emotions. Some people find listening to sad music to be helpful when processing emotion.

My experience has been that most people can't really deal with someone else's profound sadness. For example, in the United States, we live in a culture where we are told to keep busy so we can process grief. We are allowed a couple days off to attend the funeral and then it's back to business as usual. In other cultures, those who lost loved ones may mourn for months, or even a year.

Grief is a deep emotional response to a profound loss. When I was grieving the loss of my mother, I was fortunate that one person shared how an experience with grief can be viewed as a loving reflection of how much a person meant to us. Even though the deceased continue to be a presence in our lives, they are no longer available to us on a physical plane. We need to process the change and loss.

View grieving as healing. Go through the process and don't allow anyone to diminish or rush your feelings. My belief is that people want us to move on because it's uncomfortable for them to see our suffering. Suffering and feeling the emotions is the only way to truly overcome grief and sadness. Once you've processed these heavy emotions on a deep level, a sense of true freedom will prevail.

Guilt and Shame

Feelings of guilt and shame can cause an overabundance of pain. These feelings tend to eat away at the core of our being. It's hard to love or forgive yourself if you're carrying around these negative emotions.

Guilt can be beneficial when we compare actions to our personal values. The discomfort may facilitate a positive change or at least some self-reflection. If you've made mistakes that caused harm to yourself or others, the reflection may allow for apologies to be made.

If a situation calls for making amends, work toward that by reaching out and acknowledging the wrongdoings so that you can move on. Unresolved guilt gets in the way of making clear decisions. So learn from your mistakes and move forward in a positive manner.

Shame can be more damaging than guilt as it can create feelings of unworthiness and lowered self-esteem. Shame is all about those unwritten rules that you have created for yourself. If not handled, it can lead to self-neglect and sabotage or even extreme perfectionism. Watch out for all the "shoulds" you demand of yourself as they can lead to unrealistic expectations. Practice self-compassion. Learn to forgive and accept any imperfections.

Shame causes us to feel something is wrong with us. As children, we may have been taught to be ashamed of our mistakes, actions or emotions, and over time, we develop a fear of ridicule over missteps. Although it may be challenging, when someone is trying to make you feel ashamed, respond to them in an assertive, confident manner. The more that you practice this, the easier it will become to dismiss critical comments and negative voices and stories that may have been playing in your head for years.

Loneliness

Loneliness can be tied to the quality of a relationship as well as the absence of a relationship. Even though I was in a long-term marriage, I still felt a profound and deep sense of loneliness because of a lack of connectedness. We can be surrounded by people and still feel lonely.

Loneliness has been linked to a variety of health conditions including heart disease, diabetes and arthritis. But how do we overcome loneliness?

One thing to consider is that you can't feel lonely if you like the person you're with, and no matter your circumstances, the person always around is yourself. Yes, you have to like yourself.

I've found that little things, anything that can provide a glimmer of hope, are helpful when trying to beat loneliness. Sunlight provides that for me. A walk on the beach, stargazing or some time in nature can help, even if it's in your own backyard. A workout may be the key to lifting your spirits. Everyone is different. Find those little things that can lift you up, even if it's just a tiny bit.

Most of all, notice your self defeating thoughts. My perceived loneliness was a result of remaining in a relationship that was unfulfilling. Once I left my marriage and started to rebuild my self-love and confidence blocks, I realized that I was just creating a story that wasn't real. I believed that I was unworthy of love, which was definitely not the case. If you try to find tools to help, but are still feeling trapped in this emotion, be sure to reach out for help.

During our lifetimes, we will all experience undesirable emotions, but remember you have the ability to shift your thoughts and get to a different state of mind. Understanding and processing negative emotions is necessary to achieve a healthy mindset. Journaling is one way to process some emotions. Putting pen to paper allows those feelings to flow through the body and onto the page.

Practice mindfulness. Focus only on current feelings, not incidents that happened in the past and not the worries of the future. Recognize the negative consequences of holding on to the past and let it go.

When we dwell in negative spaces too long, we end up operating on autopilot or feeling broken. I'd compare myself to Humpty Dumpty as I fell apart and broke into pieces after my ended marriage. Fortunately, over time, I've been able to collect the pieces and put myself back together again. It's not all bad to lose a sense of self-identity for a short time. Transformation occurs when you put the pieces back in the right places and become strong and empowered. Let it hurt and then let it go.

CHAPTER 20

NOBODY'S PERFECT

As humans we are all perfectly imperfect. We all have good qualities, such as being thoughtful and loving or courageous and calm, but we can't always operate at a level of perfection, so cut yourself some slack. If you don't give yourself some grace, your self-esteem and confidence are sure to collapse.

The definition of self-esteem is having confidence in one's own worth or abilities. It denotes one's self-respect. The definition of self-confidence is a feeling of trust in one's abilities, qualities and judgment.

Self-confidence allows us to experience the feeling of being complete. You'll have a sense of inner peace when you trust yourself and have control of your life. Many people, even if they appear to be confident individuals, struggle with these concepts. Fashion magazines and social media have made sure that we can't measure up to others' successes in some areas.

One of the simplest ways to work on building confidence and esteem is to listen to how you talk to yourself. Pay attention to your typical thoughts or the negative things that you regularly say. Don't accept these as truths and reframe them to positive statements as soon as you catch yourself.

Another way, which I've mentioned previously, and can't stress enough, is don't compare yourself to anyone else. When you find yourself doing this, shift your perspective and focus on the things that you're grateful for in life. Try to ditch the "lacking" attitude focusing on the many blessings in your life. Focus on your goals and accomplishments.

Talk to yourself in the manner you would speak to your children or someone you love dearly. You would not speak harshly to them about similar circumstances, so give yourself the same grace.

Don't dwell in the past. Don't relive the good old days and definitely don't stay stuck in the muck of yesterday or yesteryears. Practice mindfulness and focus on the present moment. Don't pay attention to negative voices in your head.

Boosting confidence takes some self-evaluation. Take a close look at your inner circle, which includes your family and close friends. Make sure that you're surrounding yourself with people who build your confidence and not those who put you down. Instead of dwelling on the problems in your life, begin to look for positive solutions. If you're surrounded by positive people, it will be easier to implement ways to boost esteem and confidence.

The only way to fail is to give up so don't give up. Shut down negative thought patterns and refuse to accept failure. Again, if you haven't failed many times in life, chances are that you're probably not living. Analyze your successes and make a list if that helps. The list can serve as motivation on days when you're needing a boost.

One of the main problems for folks who are lacking the confidence is that they don't focus enough on themselves. They are more focused on others' judgments and how they are viewed. A lack of confidence or esteem can negatively affect all areas of your life, from relationships to career choices.

The simplest way to rebuild confidence blocks is by believing in yourself. Sounds easy enough, right? Having faith that you can get things done requires the belief that failure is not a possibility. It requires an "I can" attitude. There's no room to think, "This is too hard" or I can't," as those fears and insecurities seep in and stifle any chance for success. If this is all new to you, be sure to set small and achievable goals in the beginning.

Begin to slowly rewrite your story. We all have the story that we have created about ourselves. Our perceptions and beliefs evolve from the story. Negative self-talk is repeated so much that we believe the story saying "I'm fat," "I'm so stupid" or "I'll never amount to anything," even if it's not true. These automatic thoughts that were instilled at some point during your character development need to be unlearned and replaced with positive affirmations. Treat yourself with kindness, encouragement and compassion. You may want to consider areas or situations in your life that worked well. Focus on the positive manner in which you handled successful endeavors.

We tend to be our worst critics, so remember that when it comes to self worth, only one opinion matters, and that's yours.

CHAPTER 21

MOMENT BY MOMENT

Now that we've talked about the importance of building self-esteem and confidence, let's take a look at slowing down and appreciating each and every moment.

It's challenging to stay in a mindful state, enjoying each moment, because we are accustomed to looking at the rewards of the future or cannot shake the misery of the past. When we get immersed in the future or the past, we forget to simply enjoy what's happening right now. The danger of not living for the moment is reaching that state of sleepwalking through life, where we feel numb, as if we are operating on autopilot.

It's natural to dream about what's next. When we are dealing with the doldrums of the workweek, we are doing a countdown until the weekend, letting the hours, moments and seconds get away and not taking notice of the beauty life has to offer. We dream about vacation or worry about not meeting deadlines, or simply that we are not doing enough. If we get stuck mulling over the negativity of past experiences and struggles or get too attached to future outcomes, we lose our sense of peace and can't live in the here and now.

A lot of us tend to wait until each New Year's Eve to make shifts or resolutions that often fall by the wayside a few months into the year. We wait until Mondays to start that healthy eating plan or to begin workouts.

In the past, when I made an unhealthy food choice, I'd make a second decision that my resolve was ruined so I should just continue on my unhealthy path the rest of the day and start over the next day. A better thing to do in such a situation would be to make a healthy choice the next time I ate a meal or snack.

Although human nature causes us to make a clean, precise start, the fact is that we can start over at any moment. Change doesn't have to be restricted to the start of the year, the week or the moment you wake up. A do-over can take place any time. Even now as you read and absorb this. You are taking a step toward changing your life. Isn't that a wonderful concept?

We are always only a thought or decision away from a different life or situation. Living moment by moment allows you to remain in a state of positivity since you're not dwelling on the shortcomings of yesterday, and the fear or the future is not holding you back. All we have is the present moment to enjoy in all its glory.

Yet, beautiful moments in life are often drowned out when fears and anxiety take the wheel. Spiritual teacher Eckhart Tolle explained it well: "Stress is caused by being 'here' but wanting to be 'there.'"

Unfortunately, wanting to be any place other than where we are in our current state will take us away from living in the moment. We often live our lives in a state of distraction. It's not easy to live in the here and now since there's always something that we need to prepare for and reliving the past is commonplace. Our busy, well-planned lives are often filled with anxiety and an abundance of stress. Being mindful of what's happening in each moment is vital to stay in the present. If you can manage your thoughts, happiness is much more accessible because you can be more grounded and connected, which can lead to better health.

Technology that allows us to document every moment or sends us alerts via social media platforms make it harder to stay present. And it's impossible not to visit the past and future with our thoughts. Sometimes it's a wise or healthy choice to do so. It really comes down to balancing your thoughts of the past, present and future. Focusing your awareness on the present instead of the future can definitely reduce worry. And if you're not focused on failures, the burdens of the past can be lightened.

Mindfulness is needed to live moment to moment, and its key components are awareness and acceptance. Awareness allows us to focus on our experiences and inner feelings. Acceptance allows us to accept the experiences without judgment. When we view situations without judgment, it allows us to observe the situation or feelings with clarity instead of emotion.

An example is the negative effects of stuffing emotions, as I used food to fill voids instead of sitting with the pain. Mindfulness can be especially helpful when we are faced with pain we want to avoid. When we avoid pain, it can lead to deeper distress.

Take a moment to sit and mentally scan your body. Examine the feelings or sensations inside yourself. When we acknowledge negative emotions and how it may be affecting us physically, it allows us to work through them. We can get to a point where we can move forward.

Whenever you're feeling anxious or worried about the future or fretting about past experiences, focus on taking deep breaths. Pay attention to the act of inhaling and exhaling. This moment of calm will bring you back to the present moment.

Think of some common everyday occurrences that may be holding you back on a regular basis. How many of us are dreading the start of the workweek to the point we can't enjoy the weekend or even time with our kids? When working on a project, do you enjoy the process or is the end result and getting it finished that takes over your mind? Are you so caught up in past experiences that you are missing out on new or current opportunities that would allow you to thrive? Are you allowing the opinions of others to keep you in place?

If we're not mindful, thoughts and emotions can control and consume us.

Setting small achievable goals can help if you're a planner, like myself. Goals and intentions are wonderful and sometimes necessary. Just remember to be mindful if you are getting drawn into negativity of self-doubt. Remember that you're in control; and if you change your thoughts, it can change your life.

We've all experienced those moments of flow when everything magically works out. This happens when we are so engrossed in an event or activity that we lose track of everything else. You're so focused that distractions are not a possibility or reality and you're unaware of the passage of time. For me, creating artwork, especially paintings, took me to this state. I could be working on a canvas for more than four hours that felt like mere minutes. Painting sessions were welcomed during times of stress as they would whisk me away and allow me to enjoy the moment-by-moment process.

Find some activities that allow you to get lost in the moment. Bask in the happiness and joy that simple activities can offer. Whatever you decide to do, commit to being there wholeheartedly. We are always rushing to get to the next thing. We can all relate to the statements of, "I'll be happy when this happens…" but then when something does come to fruition, we realize that the end result didn't bring us the peace or happiness that we desired, and we begin yet another search for satisfaction. Through my trials and tribulations, I've learned that the journey is what's important. Each step that we take to reach our goals is more exciting than the end result, so relish the moments, enjoy the journey, and just be.

CHAPTER 22

FOCUS ON NEXT STEPS

At my lowest points, as I sat with myself, moving forward seemed impossible. Jumping off a rock ledge was an attractive choice because it could not feel worse than the pain I felt. As I began to resurface with the help of some tools that I've shared and with the help of supportive individuals, I came to realize that I alone am responsible for my own happiness. Nothing outside of myself was going to provide the peace I was seeking.

I'd been informed before that each of us is responsible for our own happiness and well-being. It's hard to accept this as truth when we are taught from childhood to seek others who complete us; acting as if we aren't born whole to begin with. If we keep looking for external things to make us happy, we will be continually disappointed because true happiness comes from within oneself.

Slowly but surely, I began to make small changes in my life that added up to big changes. An outing to the beach, meditation, eating healthier, going to sleep a bit earlier all added up when it came to wellness, emotionally and physically.

The health of the different layers or our bodies—physical, mental, emotional and spiritual—contribute to our well-being. By making adjustments in these four areas, focusing on and attending to personal needs, it's easy to feel more balanced and whole. This self-care is the groundwork for self-love.

Self-care involves intention, planning and taking the time to attend to your basic physical, mental, emotional and spiritual needs. Finding harmony between the four bodies is important because stress occurs when our needs are unmet. If you practice mindfulness, you will know what is most helpful at the time. Maybe you need more play and creativity, or it could be that sitting quietly in prayer and meditation is the perfect choice of nourishment. The situation doesn't need to necessarily be uplifting but maybe it's necessary to sit with something unpleasant, feeling the emotions and processing them, so that you can let go. Here's some tips on dealing with the four body systems:

The Physical Body

Our physical bodies allow us to move about and survive in the world. Actions associated with maintaining a healthy body include a proper diet and nutrition, engaging in regular workouts and getting adequate rest. Being active is one of the steps that you can take to ensure that you're living your best life. When focusing on improvement in the physical body, consider finding fun ways to move the body. It's more likely that you'll stay active and exercise more if you're engaged in activities that you enjoy, whether it's dancing and yoga, or tennis or interval training. Spending time in nature also has benefits, so outdoor activities provide good options. Listen to your body and don't compare yourself to others.

Eating healthy looks different for each of us but planning healthy meals fits into all of the different categories. If you fail to plan, plan to fail. If meals are planned and prepared and healthy snacks are available, it will be easier to stay on course. Guilt and shame are emotions that can wreak havoc on the physical body, so if you have treats or cheat days, enjoy them and get back on track when you're ready. Beating yourself up can be a recipe for disaster and can create setbacks. Start making small changes that add up over time. Add a rainbow of fruits, vegetables and whole grains into your diet.

Sleep is typically one of the first things to fall by the wayside when our schedule gets hectic. In a world where we are constantly on the go, it's important to press the pause button so that we can relax and reset. Don't skimp on sleep and your body will thank you. If you're looking for better sleep, consider a bedtime routine. Reduce your screen time. Find some soothing activities to do like a warm bath or a relaxing meditation to clear the mind.

The Mental Body

The mental body is responsible for your thoughts, goals, beliefs, morals and desires. If you don't keep this body in check, it could really hold you back. Begin by eliminating stressors in your life so that it's easier to make more thoughtful and wise decisions. Stress fogs up the mind but also can present undesirable physical reactions in the body.

Inspirational books and classes can help in this arena if that's something relatable. The mental body can be rigid and if beliefs and values do not align, you can end up feeling stuck. The responsibilities of the mental body provide the foundation of manifestation and attaining goals.

Consider setting achievable goals. Find someone to help you be accountable to your goals if that helps.

When the mind isn't connected and flowing with the rest of the body, it can keep us stuck in past patterns. The mind is responsible for the discernment of information. It's important to be able to think clearly so it's possible to continue to gain knowledge and wisdom.

Keep your mind active, seek out problem-solving activities and learning opportunities to stay sharp.

The Emotional Body

Past fears can create future anxiety because the emotional body holds all of the emotions from our past experiences. Sadness and grief, jealousy, guilt, shame, resentment, anger and fears are stored in the body and control how you respond to current situations. They create a type of blueprint in the body that people often refer to as baggage. If emotions are not worked through, it may resurface in different scenarios throughout a lifetime until they are finally addressed. We need good emotional intelligence to maintain healthy relationships.

Forgiveness is critical. If you didn't get that after reading Chapter 14, go back and reread that section. Remember that forgiveness is for your benefit. Let me repeat that...forgiveness is for your own well-being. Some people and situations may not deserve your forgiveness, but by forgiving and letting go, they no longer have a hold on you. The longer you hold on, it's as if you've handed your power over to another person or situation.

Adopt an attitude of gratitude. If you can stay in a place of gratitude, it's easier to contain your emotions. A fun dinner activity is to take turns and share your highlights of the day with family or friends, or share three things that you're thankful for that day. Keeping a personal gratitude journal helps you focus on the positive things in life. If you're not one to journal, typing notes on your phone works. But I think that the thoughts and awareness are the critical components even if nothing is written or spoken, since some of us don't need more tasks or "to do" items.

Make relationships a priority and that includes the relationship with yourself. Surround yourself with positive people who uplift you. People will always have negative things to say. Those who judge and criticize others are normally not happy in their own lives. Loving others is easy when you love and accept yourself.

When we maintain a positive outlook and keep emotions in check, well-being increases, resulting in better physical health and creating harmony in all four bodies.

The Spiritual Body

Everything around us, including ourselves, is composed of energy. The spiritual body connects us to the energy of all things. We experience conflict and struggle when we are feeling disconnected. Seeking the deeper meaning or life and purpose may create an internal struggle. Being connected to source is of the utmost importance. Remember this can range from God to your higher self or nature. Anything that helps with your connection to source will contribute to better health and well-being.

Like everything else, you'll need to explore what works best for you. Consider adopting a daily meditation practice or at least spend some time alone in reflection. Practicing mindfulness helps us to stay present in the here and now. It keeps us from worrying about the future or fretting about the past.

Prayer provides a powerful connection for some people. I've participated in ceremonies and even mastermind groups where the collective is focused on the same outcomes of holding space for those involved. I've seen things come to fruition through this process, so for me, it's on my spiritual "to do" list.

Energy work has opened my eyes to the endless possibilities that are available to us. I've learned several modalities, which have allowed me to tap into the energies around me. I've found that helps me to be more in tune with myself and my surroundings.

Finding that connection may require learning some stress reduction techniques. Taking a few deep breaths provides a simple way of calming yourself down.

Just because you do these things and find a sense of connectedness, it doesn't mean that you won't experience conflict, but a strong spiritual foundation makes it easier to handle things that come your way.

We are on this planet to heal and grow, and help others do the same. Working through the pain and owning up to truths can lead you on a path of healing and spiritual growth. All that you need to have or everything you want to have resides inside you right now. Keep your eyes and heart open and experience all of the whimsy, wonder and magic that life has to offer.

CHAPTER 23

FIND YOUR TRIBE

Simply put, without my tribe, I wouldn't survive.

My tribe acts as a support system and provides care and reinforcement in times of need. It's composed of people who respect you. They uplift you and don't judge you.

My support system kept me afloat during some of my darkest days. From basic needs of food and shelter to providing a listening ear, hand holding and picking me up off the ground, my tribe was there for me.

Finding your people is of the utmost importance. Your tribe will always accept you as you are. It's important to surround yourself with those folks who help you to become the best version of yourself. The tribe will celebrate your successes and lift you when you're feeling down.

When I left my house and was waiting for my ex-boyfriend to make arrangements for my move, I had nowhere to go. A friend allowed me to stay in her home until the time came to make the big leap and move. My ex-boyfriend held up the move for a year, taking a couple of short-term jobs on the island so we could be together. I found out right before the break-up, that in between his island stops, he had been taking jobs where his other girlfriend lived. I'd be loyally awaiting his return at this friend's home. Thankfully she patiently let everything unfold as it did. Otherwise, on top of my future being on hold, I'd have required looking for another temporary place of residence. My tribe kept my spirits up during these challenging times.

When I returned to Hawaii after the betrayal, another dear friend opened up her home and let me just be and heal and expected absolutely nothing in return. I spent days on end crying in my room. Sometimes it was challenging to breathe. She made sure that I was OK without infringing on my space and healing. Honestly, I can say without a doubt, that I don't think I would have remained on this earth if it weren't for her loving kindness.

I didn't want to go anywhere but another friend would drag me to the beach or on a walk at least once a week. I was definitely not good company but she didn't care. She continued to regularly pick me up and made sure that I had sunshine, love and support.

I didn't have much hope and wasn't able to count my blessings during these times, but these beautiful souls remained faithful. I'm eternally grateful for the loving kindness that I received and continue to receive on a daily basis. Once I could resurface a bit, laughing with my friends was a treasured experience.

They put up with ugly cries and angry outbursts. They endured my never-ending pain for months on end. When I finally got to the other side, my tribe was cheering me on. I'd finally made it.

Reaching out and asking for support is not always easy to do. It was mind-boggling that people would want ro spend time with me in that state. I was so wrong because true friends aren't looking for a certain mood to be in your company. Sure, we would all prefer less drama and to laugh and be happy, but helping someone get to the other side of things can be equally fulfilling.

I'd forgotten that in my downtrodden state. These folks loved me when I couldn't love myself. They lifted me up when it seemed impossible. They held space for me and allowed me to see a flicker of hope when darkness was all that there was in view.

Be yourself if you're searching for the right tribe members. Maintain friendships that make you feel comfortable. These tribe members will love you when you're unable to love yourself.

Again, it's important to surround yourself with folks who encourage you to be the best version of yourself. I'd define a tribe as people who share similar values and interests, but before you find your tribe, you really need to know yourself. If you don't truly see yourself and know your core, it will be challenging to find the people who serve us best in life. Once you're comfortable in your own skin, you'll attract people who have the qualities that you're looking for in a friend. They will meet the ideals of what's important to you.

For instance, is it important that friends or members of your support team are good listeners? Are you seeking knowledge or advice to get you to the next level? Maybe you're looking for emotional support. Whatever the case, practice finding those qualities in yourself so that it's easier to attract these people into your life. Core friendships are easier to form with like-minded folks. Similar values can help when it comes to accountability, which we all need.

During my young and formative years, I never really fit in. During high school, my friendship pool was colorful and filled with some party animals, jocks and studious nerds. They all sort of accepted me but I didn't truly belong or feel fully comfortable. This scenario continued into adulthood. Although I had plenty of friends, they were all from diverse backgrounds and I didn't feel a solid fit. After doing lots of soul-searching during challenging times in the past decade, I've finally found my people and it feels much easier. It took really knowing myself to find the right fit. So take some quiet time to contemplate your desires, what friendship means to you and set intentions to attract the right people into your life at the right times.

I absolutely love people. One of my closest friends always asks me how I haven't managed to lose faith in humanity when so much has happened during my lifetime that could have left me bitter.

I suppose that I see a glimpse of myself in everyone I meet, whether it's acknowledging a place where I was once stuck or seeing a place where I'm heading. That said, I choose to keep my love vibe going. I'd rather be a beacon of light for others and not bring any more darkness into the world. We tend to have enough shadow area and darkness in our own lives to contend with and don't need extra.

You'll probably find your tribe will be ever-changing as you grow and move through life. Be reminded that some people are tribe members forever and others may just be there for a reason or a season. The temporary tribe members are equally important. They may just be there to help get you through something with shared experiences or to learn a life lesson that allows you to grow and evolve. The same goes for you when you're a part of someone's tribe. We all change and grow, so don't take it personally if or when things end.

One friend offered some profound advice: "Only have someone in your life if they add to yours."

Some tips on finding your tribe:

1. Know yourself. Take a look inside yourself and know what you desire, your passions, likes and dislikes. Be your authentic self. Once you've established who you are and how you fit into the world, attracting other like-minded people will be much easier.
2. Love yourself. Or I should say, like yourself. Delve deep and find the self-worth and confidence that you deserve in life. When you're in your low moments, the tribe will be able to hold you up and uplift you so that you can get back to this space.
3. Stop being superficial. Get rid of judgments if you want to find kindred spirits. I've learned not to judge a book by its cover. The contents inside may pleasantly surprise you. Spend time paying attention to whether or not you resonate with a person on a deeper level. Make an effort to really get to know someone.
4. Build relationships. If you're on autopilot or flying under the radar to avoid conflict or undesirable emotions, don't

expect friends to step up to the plate when you need them. Giving and receiving is a beautiful exchange of energy. Be kind and open.

5. Ending friendships is perfectly fine. Remove people from your life who do not bring you happiness and joy. Get rid of the friends who don't allow you to be your authentic self. Love them from afar. End those friendships where you feel judged. If someone is not rooting for you to live a good life, they probably don't deserve a spot in your line-up. Removing these undesirable relationships will open more space for the like-minded tribe members that you're seeking in life.

CHAPTER 24

THE NEVERENDING JOURNEY: THE MAINTENANCE PHASE

The good news is that you've got this! The bad news is that it's a continual and lifelong process.

My belief is that all healing is self-healing. Sure there are facilitators and conduits that help along the way, whether it's doctors, therapists or alternative healers, but in order for us to actually grow or even begin to heal, we have to first believe that it's possible.

So believe!

Believe in the power that resides inside of you. Believe in and witness everyday miracles. Let go of the things that no longer serve you in order to create the life that you deserve. Bring your deepest desires to fruition.

Human nature is to give to others even if it means neglecting our own needs. We are taught that it's selfish to put our own needs before others' so most people plug away, continuing to serve others without a thought of caring for themselves. Begin the process of making yourself a priority. There's a reason that in case of emergencies, airline personnel instruct you to put your oxygen mask on before helping others. If you aren't OK, it's difficult to help anyone else. When we are running on empty, we don't really have much to offer.

So take time for yourself. Time is our most valuable commodity. Once it's given away, it can't be replenished. You can make money and replace things, but you can't get time back.

Make sure that your cup is full. Be sure that you're loving yourself enough to fulfill your own needs before you give to others. You'll be so much more effective if you can make this a habit.

We have years of education but no one taught us how to love ourselves and why it's so important. In order to fill up, ask yourself if you're feeding your mind, body and spirit what it needs.

Check in and make sure that you are speaking kindly to yourself. Are you following through with a self-care routine? Are you letting your needs fall by the wayside because you're not making yourself a priority and practicing self-love?

Once you begin to cultivate and maintain a deep sense of self-love, that light will emanate out into the world and everyone that you encounter.

So what are you waiting for? Go out and have a love affair with yourself. You'll be glad you did.

I'm still living out of my two suitcases and a carry-on bag but life is absolutely beautiful. For months, they were a burden on my psyche; a grand reminder of my deep pain and despair.

But now when I look at them, I smile; the same way I smiled at lost love. These pieces of luggage represent my journey and how far I've come. Now I can look at them with a sense of adventure and ponder the grand adventures that await me.

THE ROAD FORWARD

*"The only person you are destined to become
is the person you decide to be."*
– Ralph Waldo Emerson

TIPS, CHECKLISTS AND WRITING PROMPTS

Self-love is a continual process. It's easier if you can find a routine and practices that keep you focused. The following pages include tips, checklists and writing prompts that can help you along the way to well-being and living the life that you desire and deserve. Love is the answer. Self-love and unconditional love for others brings about spiritual growth, and promotes well-being. Please take notes and start a passionate love affair with yourself! Find the joy. It's waiting for you.

TAKE TIME TO DECLUTTER

As mentioned in Chapter 3, decluttering involves sorting, organizing, decision making and disposing of the things that are no longer needed or wanted. It's a matter of going through your belongings and deciding what will be thrown away, recycled or kept. For some, it can be a grueling and emotionally charged process. It's not just physical things that you'll be sorting through. Our possessions are often connected to an array of emotions that may come rushing to the surface. Allow these moments to propel you forward. They can be a catalyst that allows you to grow and flourish. Take stock of your emotions or stimuli that are holding you back, as well.

Despite the emotions that crept in during my personal purge, I highly recommend decluttering on a regular basis. Here's some decluttering tips:

Physical

1. Set-up three bins for sorting items: one for items to recycle and donate; one for trash and another for things to keep.
2. Remember that most items will have some sort of memory or sentimental value attached. When choosing to keep

items, only pick those that bring you joy. Purge any items that you don't use.

3. Take photographs of the items that you can't keep.
4. Once you've finished getting rid of the clutter, apply a rule that you can't buy or have another item until you get rid of one that's already in your home. This rule will keep you organized and save you money.
5. Allow the emotions to flow as you part with the past.

Emotional and Mental

1. Let go of things, people and situations that no longer serve your well-being.
2. Journal your thoughts. Get it down on paper. Release any negative thoughts that are weighing you down. A fire-burning ritual can provide a cathartic healing experience. Writing down those things that no longer serve you and watching those words melt away in the fire, turning to ash, has been helpful in my experience.
3. Practice forgiveness. Remember that forgiving someone does not mean that you're dismissing their actions. Hanging on to anger and resentment hurts you, so forgiveness is beneficial for your well-being. Make it a regular priority to forgive yourself. Self-forgiveness is often the hardest form of forgiveness. Give yourself lots of grace.
4. Be mindful of old patterns and limiting beliefs. Let them go! Do everything in your power to release beliefs that hold you back.
5. Words are powerful, so choose them wisely. Remember that you can either hurt or uplift someone with words. Consider removing should, can't, try and any words that leave us feeling guilty or contribute to negative stories that we tell ourselves.

Spiritual

1. Spiritual clutter is lack of peace; lack of contentment; and lack of forgiveness. Adapt an attitude of gratitude.
2. Detach from too much stimuli. Take a break from social media and electronics.
3. Pray and/or meditate. If nothing else, find some alone time for quiet contemplation.
4. Practice mindfulness. In our busy lives, it's easy to get sucked into multitasking and not fully be present in any activity.
5. Experience the benefits of letting go.

SELF LOVE FOR SURVIVAL

A simple way to get and stay on track is by having some basic survival skills. It's easy to get dragged down by emotions or undesirable situations or encounters. The main goal is always self-love. By focusing on self-love and practicing mindfulness, it can help you stay in a space of gratitude and steer clear of fears and doubts.

Some Basic Survival Tips

1. Love yourself. I mean really love yourself. Be gentle, honor your feelings and work through the emotions at your own pace
2. Live in the moment. Take things one day at a time. When life knocks you down, thinking about the future can be overwhelming, so live in the here and now. The current moment is all you have.
3. Know that you're never alone.
4. Create a support system.
5. Find creative outlets. Pursue your passions. Find things that make your heart sing.
6. Seek out solace in nature. Find your happy place. Those settings that bring you joy also bring about a sense of peace.

7. Feed yourself in a healthy manner, body, mind and spirit. It's not just the food that we put into our body that matters. We need to continually assess our thoughts and emotions, too.

Personal Self Care Plan

As I mentioned on numerous occasions, it's easy for us to help others and neglect our own needs. Make a checklist of things that would nourish you, and keep you healthy in body, mind and spirit. Do at least one thing on the list everyday. Here's a sample list:

1. Get in a workout whether it's a short walk or interval training If inspired, dance around the living room to your favorite tunes.
2. Spend some time in nature, at the beach or park, or anywhere that promotes a sense of relaxation.
3. Meditate at least 10 minutes each day.
4. Take a soothing bath. Use essential oils and lotions. Do those things that feel pampering.
5. Write, draw, paint, dance or engage in activities that allow for creativity.
6. Watch your favorite movies or videos or listen to a fun podcast.
7. Spend time with people who uplift you.

Remember that you can make a long list and it doesn't mean that you have to do each item on a daily basis. It's just good to have a list to draw from when you're in a space where you need a pick-me-up or have been neglecting your needs. If you can remain in a loving heart based space, you'll see that it's much easier to manifest the things that you desire in life.

BECOME A MASTER OF MANIFESTATION

Manifestation is an important element of creating the life of your dreams. Manifestation is the act of bringing something tangible into your life through attraction and belief. Limiting beliefs can interfere with the law of attraction and that makes the process of manifestation challenging. Because we are desiring one thing and holding conflicting thought patterns, attaining the goal or desire will be quite challenging.

One example would be that you have to work hard to have money. Detach from those beliefs even if something seems totally impossible. What if it was possible to pursue your passion, which wouldn't even feel like work, and make a living? Claim your worth and know that limitless possibilities are at our fingertips.

Dare to dream big! If it's something you can't imagine attaining, dream even bigger. The idea is that what you focus on will be brought into your life. Thoughts become things, so be careful what you wish for. Be mindful and choose your thoughts and words wisely. Once you've clearly decided what you want, put it out into the universe and take some action steps, but don't worry about the details. Do it scared. By taking action, you'll overcome your fears and build confidence.

Here's some things to consider when you're working on manifesting the things that you desire into your life:

1. Believe in yourself. Believe that you're worthy and deserving.
2. Decide what you want and desire. Be very clear.
3. Visualize your desire. Imagine and believe that you already have it. How does it make you feel? Use your senses to really be present with the desire.
4. Create an action plan that aligns with your desires. Write down your goals and practice gratitude.
5. Thoughts become things. Again, be careful what you wish for. Imagine that you've already attained what you want. Feel the gratitude, happiness and feelings associated now that you have exactly what you wanted.
6. Maintain a positive mindset. Doubts, worries and fears will block the manifestation process. Try to focus on gratitude whenever these negative mindsets try to take over.
7. Be prepared. Don't be afraid of obstacles.
8. Let go of any limiting beliefs that come into play so that your desires can become a reality. Dream big!

PRACTICE MINDFULNESS

Mindfulness is all about being in the present moment, so live in the moment! Focus on the here and now rather than dwelling in the past or worrying about the future.

Depending on the circumstances, living in the past can leave us feeling sad or defeated. Focusing too much about the future can have us in a state of anxiety. So take some deep breaths and practice focusing on what's happening at any specific moment. When your thoughts go awry, bring them back to the present. Mindfulness allows us to focus our awareness of what's happening at the moment and not be reactive and overwhelmed by the events in our life or what's happening around us.

Here are some suggestions on practicing mindfulness:

1. Meditation: It can be seated or walking or you could even meditate lying down. Calming the mind can help us to better focus on current situations.
2. Deep breathing: Sometimes we are challenged to leave the past or future experiences in the mind. For a few moments, focus on the breath. Focus on the inhale. Focus on the exhale. Focus on the little pause in between each

inhale and exhale. By giving yourself something to focus on, it can be easier to stay present.

3. Get moving: Practice yoga, or find a sport that demands you to keep present, like a dance class, where you need to focus to follow along and learn the steps. Mindful stretching is another option.

4. Practice the art of mindful eating: Savor each and every bite. Chew slowly and enjoy the flavors exploding in your mouth. Admire the colors on your plate or appreciate the beautiful, healthy salad that you made.

5. Get outside: Take a stroll in nature. Really notice and soak in your surroundings. Can you smell the flowers? How many different types of trees do you see? Do you see mountains or water? Are there animals that are demanding your attention? Use your senses to enjoy the magical moments in your journey.

6. Mind dump: Journaling is two-fold as far as benefits go. You can focus on the current situation and get the thoughts out of your head as they flow from pen to paper or you type them on your screen. Doing a mind dump prior to bedtime can make for a better night's rest.

These mindfulness practices are all focused on things outside ourselves. It allows us to soak in our surroundings or appreciate the quiet moments of reflection and relaxation. Anything that allows you to focus on the moment at hand will help you to make mindfulness a part of how you navigate life. Mindfulness benefits, from interpersonal to emotional, are dependent on the emphasis that's placed on establishing a daily routine, even if it's just for a few moments each day.

DAILY CHECK-IN

How are you feeling in body, mind and spirit?

I'd suggest using this as a check-in each day to see where you're at and what you need. Here are some things to consider if you're not sure how to get started.

Body: Is your body feeling achy? Are you feeling sluggish because you didn't get enough sleep? Did you skip lunch and not have enough nutrients? Do you need to drink more water? Maybe you're feeling on top of the world because you've kept up with your workouts and have been practicing good self care.

Mind: Are you feeling focused and ready for anything? Are you feeling scattered because you're being dragged into too many different directions? Are you letting fears and doubts take over? Are your emotions in check?

Spirit: Are you feeling fulfilled? Is there darkness that you need to deal with such as negative emotions that are holding you back? Are you feeling disconnected? Are you feeling connected to source? Are you a magnet for abundance?

When you can answer these questions honestly with positive responses, chances are that you're maintaining that connection to source and practicing self care. These considerations will help you keep on track. Congratulations, you've mastered the art of self-love, even if it was just for a day.

WRITING PROMPTS

Ponder these questions and explore your answers. Consider getting a journal and taking notes. These prompts are intended to allow you to dig deep and take an honest look at whether or not you've dealt with your feelings and emotions or stuffed them away.

1. Recall a time when you experienced being in a dark space? Did you hit rock bottom? What did you do to rise up and start again?

   Think about a time when you experienced adversity or hardships and avoided the downward spiral? What tools did you use to avoid turmoil? These tools and reflections may be helpful when dealing with other situations that occur in your life.

_____

_____

_____

_____

_____

_____

_____

_____

_____

_____

_____

_____

_____

2. What life events have knocked you down or left you feeling helpless? What feelings and emotions came up? Do you feel like you've worked through them or are residual feelings percolating and showing up in other areas of your life? Ponder these questions and take notes. You'll be able to gain insights to help you move through emotions and let go.

_____

_____

_____

_____

_____

_____

_____

_____

_____

_____

_____

_____

3. Recall a time when you were disillusioned by a situation? If it was in matters of the heart, express how you felt when you realized your perception was not accurate? What feelings and emotions emerged? Do you feel as if you grieved the loss completely so that you're not carrying baggage into your other relationships?

_____

_____

_____

_____

_____

_____

_____

_____

_____

_____

_____

_____

_____

4. Are you judgmental of others? Are you judgmental of yourself? When you talk to yourself, are you your best cheerleader or your harshest critic?

_____

_____

_____

_____

_____

_____

_____

_____

_____

_____

_____

_____

_____

_____

_____

5. Think about what brings you joy. Are you happy? Do you feel fulfilled? Make a list of things that would promote happiness and fulfillment in your life. Add a few new things to try.

_____

_____

_____

_____

_____

_____

_____

_____

_____

_____

_____

_____

_____

_____

6. What fears are holding you back? What are some things that you could do to face these fears and achieve your goals?

_____

_____

_____

_____

_____

_____

_____

_____

_____

_____

_____

_____

_____

_____

_____

7. Is there anyone that you need to forgive? Do you need to forgive yourself? Ponder ways that you can work on forgiveness.

_____

_____

_____

_____

_____

_____

_____

_____

_____

_____

_____

_____

_____

_____

PERSONAL ACKNOWLEDGEMENTS

There's so many people that I prefer to refer to as angels that have helped me along my path. My son John Paul, who was the absolute greatest gift in life, needs to be acknowledged by name. He has taught me so much about the world and especially about love. His humble, generous and kind-hearted soul has been and continues to be an inspiration for me. I'd be foolhardy to not express my gratitude for the blessings that his birth has provided for me.

Like everyone else, my life has been filled with both joy and sorrow but I've learned to look at all of my beautiful life as a gift. The pretty, the messy, the topsy-turvy—all of it, as an absolute blessing.

I've been down and out on more occasions than I'd care to admit. I may have lacked finances or even a roof over my head, but thankfully I was blessed with friends and beautiful people who provided me with exactly what I needed and when I needed it most. I'm not going to list names because when you're reading it, you'll know I'm talking to you and I don't want to leave anyone out. Thanks a million for the love, compassion, generosity, and beauty that you provided in my life

During my experiences of hitting rock bottom, I may not have made it through, or at least not with the same grace, without your support. During my darkest days, when I felt like I could no longer go on, one of my angels would pull me out of the pit, and lift me up enough to get through another day, or another hour or even another moment. I'm eternally grateful for these souls that allowed me to be "me" in all the darkness, ugliness and utter despair.

Thank you for allowing me the space to heal. It allowed me to heal on a deep level and not just on the surface so I could project myself as good to the outside world. I now know that I'm beautiful both inside and out. I may have pretended on many a day to get through a work shift or something else, but I'm no longer pretending. I can stand tall and be me. I'm no longer in the mindset of outward appearances. I'm confident in my skin, which is what will happen for all of you who have taken the time to read my words and apply some of the techniques to your own life.

People or situations may fall by the wayside when you step into your true self, and your true power, but it's OK. Trust in the process. There will always be angels that show up at the right time if you believe in yourself and are willing to break down the barriers. Don't hide. Go out and shine your light on the world. And remember to thank all of the angels that you encounter along the way.

PROFESSIONAL ACKNOWLEDGEMENTS

My first love affair with writing began in high school with my senior year English teacher, Mr. Hutchins. He allowed students to play with creativity and find a real passion for allowing things to flow from pen to paper. And for that, I'm eternally grateful. Without his encouragement, I may not have chosen to be a writer.

Nadine Kam, the first editor that I worked with at the newspaper, deserves props for reigniting that passion. Thanks my dear friend for forcing me out of my comfort zone on many assignments, including covering stories that had me walking on 1,200 degree coals. This allowed me to grow and flourish. You always inspire and encourage me, so thanks for being one of my longtime cheerleaders.

This book would not exist without the knowledge and wisdom that I gained from my spiritual mentors and teachers. I've been truly blessed as each of these teachers appeared in my life when I needed them the most.

Master Zhi Gang Sha, many thanks for invoking a passion within me to learn the art of self healing and helping others to heal. I adore your childlike spirit and the love you emanate into the world. You taught me that love melts all blockages, transforms all life and purifies our hearts and souls. Love is the answer. Thank you for the many blessings. I love you.

Douglas Ah Hee, your voice and wise words often pop into my head since your teachings had such a profound effect on my life. Being in your presence is healing in itself. You're definitely one of my most treasured beings. There's so much gratitude in my heart for my personal healing that you facilitated.

Pam Johnson, thank you for helping me to feel comfortable in my own skin. I loved your Reiki classes and how you opened your home for us to all practice and commune as we tapped into our intuition and became conduits for healing. Your passion and encouragement helped me to see some of the gifts that I'd been denying, which in turn has helped me to help others. We love how that happens, right?

Alan Johnson, I'm eternally grateful that you pointed out that I was carrying around an invisible backpack filled with other people's problems. Once I gave them back, I felt so much lighter! I know you're watching over us from the other side now and I'll miss your humor and wit at future gatherings. Thanks for stopping by and setting off the fire alarm in my room when I was chatting with Pam. The visit was appreciated as it provided us a reason to chuckle.

Dawn Gold, your beautiful spirit during my first Reiki class with you, enticed me to keep learning and growing. The emphasis you placed on self-care had an impact that I've continued to share with others.

Diane Hanzel, your honest and upfront approach allowed me to see the endless possibilities. Thank you for teaching me about Access Consciousness and Running the Bars. It's allowed me to help numerous people in different areas of their lives. What else is possible?

Kassia Kristoff and Glenn Jones, thank you for sharing the art of Belvaspata. Kassia, your insights and love have helped me to grow. Glenn, you showed me the importance of self-love and care.

I've learned something from everyone who has crossed my path during my lifetime. Thanks for the lessons. Thanks for the gifts. May we all continue to band together and make this world a better place. I love you all.

AFTERWORD

Embarking on a spiritual journey is not for the faint of heart. It's easier to sleepwalk through life than to reflect on ourselves and ponder how we fit into the world around us.

It's not easy to admit that you don't love, or even like, yourself. And it's often more challenging to try to give yourself the love that you deserve even though it's seemingly easy to love others.

This book has been a labor of love during my personal self-love journey. It was born as I hit rock bottom and muddled through my own healing process. My pain caused me to question how my life was evolving. It showed me how much I had been hiding and not living life. My prayer is that it may serve as a catalyst as you embark on your own personal love affair with yourself and begin to create the life that you desire and deserve.

When I was growing up, the concept of self-love was not commonly shared. It was a foreign concept that took decades to grasp and additional time to master. In fact, it was quite the opposite of my mindset. Self-criticism, shame and not feeling "good enough" was at the forefront of my life. The fact that I emerged from the darkness time and time again, until I got to a point where I could remain in the light most of the time, is remarkable. Self-love and care has helped me to get back up and stay afloat in times of chaos.

Turbulent times and hardships during my formidable years formed my belief of lack based thinking. An "I can't" attitude held me back for decades, but not anymore.

My family was poor and living on public welfare. My remarkable mother, who I can thank for my strength and resiliency, raised us as a single mom for several years with the help of my grandmother. We may have not been wealthy but there was love for one another. We always managed to have what we needed. And I cherished the second chance to have a father when my mother remarried. My stepfather was able to be a part of my milestone life events and a wonderful grandpa to my son.

Self-love may have been absent and at times, and life was challenging, but gifts arose out of all of these situations. Because I was poor, I have compassion. Because I got teased, I choose to be kind. Because I grew up in a somewhat unstable environment, I learned how to quickly read people and situations. Because I've felt abandoned, I'm loyal to a fault. Because my mother always made sure that we had everything that we needed despite the challenges, I've learned to be resourceful.

Blaming life incidents for my shortcomings or misfortunes is no longer a part of my life. I take the good and let the rest go. Self-love is the critical component.

When I was 20 years old, I left Maine, where I was born and raised, and moved to Hawaii. My best friend and I came across the "Hidden Hawaii" book and planned an imaginary grand adventure. After all of the preliminary planning, we decided to make the leap and head to the islands. It's where I've spent my adult life; it's definitely home.

Making the leap and moving back to the mainland with my ex-boyfriend was not an easy decision. It had seemed worth it because it was in the name of love. And I suppose, if I'm honest, I may have never been forced to do the deep soul-searching that's expressed in these pages if I hadn't hit rock bottom.

Undesirable things may happen, but we are always a thought or choice away from living a different life. This book definitely evolved as a result of my love affair with myself.

Amidst the chaos and melancholy, life is incredibly beautiful. May you be open to the limitless possibilities that life has to offer. Get ready and enjoy the ride. Change your thoughts and it will change your life. Love, and specifically self-love, is the answer. So open your eyes and heart and embrace the abundance of love that is all around us.

Made in the USA
Las Vegas, NV
16 March 2021

19613191R00111